C000141925

YOUR CC
COLC ᴗ⌐
DRIVING TEST
INSTRUCTOR

YOUR COMPLETE COLOUR DRIVING TEST INSTRUCTOR

by Philip Chave

foulsham

LONDON • NEW YORK • TORONTO • SYDNEY

foulsham
Yeovil Road, Slough, Berkshire SL1 4JH

ISBN 0-572-01749-9

Copyright © Philip Chave 1994

All rights reserved

The Copyright Act prohibits (subject to certain
very limited exceptions) the making of copies of any
copyright work or of a substantial part of such a work,
including the making of copies by photocopying or similar
process. Written permission to make a copy or copies must
therefore normally be obtained from the publisher in
advance. It is advisable also to consult the publisher if
in any doubt as to the legality of any copying which is
to be undertaken.

Phototypeset in Great Britain by Typesetting Solutions, Slough, Berks.
Printed in Great Britain at Cambus Litho, East Kilbride

Preface

In 1988 Philip Chave began working as a Department of Transport Approved Driving Instructor (A.D.I.), and also passed the driving test of the Institute of Advanced Motorists (I.A.M.). The same year he qualified for membership into MENSA and of British Mensa Limited.

He was prompted to write this book in an effort to help his own and other students face the unique experience of taking a driving test with the minimum of trepidation. Knowing what to expect during the test and how to reach the standard required, will go a long way towards increasing the chances of obtaining your pass certificate. By answering the questions in this book correctly, you will demonstrate to yourself that you are very conversant with the rules that govern a driver's use of the road. Reading the short passages devoted to enhancing your driving technique will help with the set test manoeuvres. Much of the information here also applies to motorists about to take their advanced driving test and go on to join the Institute of Advanced Motorists.

Born in 1958, Philip Chave lives in Somerset, and is now concentrating his efforts on writing full-time.

The author and publisher gratefully acknowledge permission by the Department of Transport and the Controller of Her Majesty's Stationery Office, to reproduce signs, rule numbers and text from 'The Highway Code', 'Know Your Traffic Signs' and 'Your Driving Test'.

Philip Chave, 1994

Contents

Introduction

The average new motorist has but one goal: to pass the driving test. A worthwhile ambition indeed!

This is only the first stage in learning to drive — there is more to motoring that just passing a test. The sad fact remains that, all too often, the fairly basic standard required becomes increasingly eroded until it bears little resemblance to even the minimum 'pass' requirement. Equally, the fact that over half of the candidates who take the test each year fail, shows that many apply who are just not ready to drive unsupervised.

This book has been especially designed, with questions and answers, to help you develop a sound theoretical base for driving on the road, to provide a comprehensive insight into the rules of the *Highway Code* and the reasoning behind them. It only remains that you incorporate these rules into your driving technique and practise until you are sure you can apply them safely, thereby coaching yourself to a standard higher than the official test. The final chapter deals with the actual test requirements and the examiner's expectations of your competence. This will enable you to approach your test with a positive frame of mind; the test itself, just confirmation of your own assurance.

Through this book, I hope to promote in learners and other motorists the valuable characteristics of a really good driver. These include: *responsibility* and *safety,* for ourselves and others, *knowledge, patience, concentration, skill, positioning, anticipation, awareness* and *confidence.*

With these qualities readily available and the chance to acquire practical experience, you can make driving a pleasure and take pride in your ability to do something really well, sure in the knowledge that you are contributing to safer motoring.

1

The Meaning of the Highway Code

Q What is the point of the Highway Code?

A. The Highway Code is a system of rules, that, if adhered to by everyone, gives each of us a good chance of getting from one place to another, on foot or by mechanical means, safely and in the least amount of time. It is a teaching aid for pedestrians and drivers which helps us all to use the complex road system carefully.

Q The Highway Code is issued under whose authority? Underline. 1. The Police Force. 2. The Department of Transport. 3. The RAC and AA. 4. Parliament. 5. The Transport Secretary. 6. The Home Office.

A. 4. Parliament.

FACT: *A failure on the part of a person to observe the provision of the Highway Code shall not, of itself, render that person liable to criminal proceedings, but, it can be used to establish or negate liability of infractions in those proceedings.*

Q Why do you need to study the Highway Code for your test?

A. Because I must satsify the examiner that I not only have a good understanding of driving technique, but can also recognise, understand and adopt the correct action on all other aspects of driving, such as, road markings, traffic lights, signs, pedestrian crossings, the signals of other road users, my safety and the margins I allow others who are potentially at risk by my actions.

2

*P*edestrians Walking Along the Road

FACT: *It makes sense that if there is a pavement to walk on, you should use it. If possible avoid walking next to the kerb with your back to the traffic. If you need to pass an obstruction in the town centre (people chatting, etc) ask to be let by instead of stepping down into the gutter. You may well be hit by a passing car or make the driver swerve into someone else. Otherwise, if you have to step into the road, have a good look around for vehicles first.* **Rule 1**

 Where there is no pavement, for example, on country roads, which side of the road should you walk on?

A. The right hand side, facing oncoming traffic. This means that I must take extra care when approaching right hand bends and especially on narrow roads or in poor light walk in single file, listening carefully. *Rule 2*

 When walking with children, underline the points you feel are relevant. 1. Don't allow children under five out alone. 2. Walk between them and the traffic. 3. Hold their hand. 4. Use reins or a pushchair.

A. I am responsible for the safety of my children, so all the points are relevant, depending on their ages. *Rule 4*

 How can you protect yourself when walking at night?

A. I should wear something light or reflective. Bright armbands, sold for cyclists, are cheap and equally as effective for pedestrians when worn over ordinary clothes. I could carry a newspaper or white supermarket bag.
Rule 3

FACT: *Fluorescent objects or material are of little value in the dark. Wear reflective armbands, sashes or other material instead.* *Rule 3*

Q Underline whichever of the following you think are correct: What should groups of people walking or marching along the roadside do: 1. Keep to the left. 2. Keep to the right. 3. Post a lookout at the back. 4. Post a lookout in front. 5. Both 3 and 4. 6. Wear a uniform. 7. Wear something reflective at night. 8. Carry lights at night (white in front, red at the back. The light at the back should be visible from behind). 9. Carry amber lights.

A. 1, 5, 7 and 8. *Rule 5*

Q What does this sign mean?

A. No pedestrians allowed.

Crossing the Road

Q The Green Cross Code is a guide for who? Tick one. 1. Children. 2. Pensioners. 3. Car drivers. 4. Pedestrians.

A. It is a guide for all pedestrians (4), to enable them to cross the road in safety. *Rule 7*

FACT: *The Green Cross Code entails judging the speed and distance of approaching vehicles before crossing. The Highway Code states that many children under ten cannot judge how fast vehicles are going or how far away they are. However, the age of understanding is different for each child. So as soon as your children can walk beside you, teach them by example and use the Code in full yourself.* *Rule 7*

Q What is the first thing you should do before crossing?

A. Think to myself 'Is this a safe place to cross?' *Rule 7a*

11

Give sensible answers to each of the following questions.
1. Where is it safest to cross?
2. Where is it least safe to cross?
3. How close to the kerb should you stand?
4. Before crossing what should you do?
5. Should you be ready to run if necesssary?
6. Once you've started to cross, why should you keep looking?

A. 1. At subways, footbridges, islands, Zebra crossings, Pelican crossings, traffic lights, where the police, a school patrol or traffic warden are controlling, or where I can see clearly in all directions. (Did you get them all?)   *Rule 7a*
2. Between parked cars (Rule 7a & Rule 23) or near a bend.
3. I should compromise between seeing clearly and putting myself at risk perhaps by being jostled forward off the kerb. I can stop a little way back.   *Rule 7b*
4. Stop — Look — Listen. I should look all around for traffic and listen very carefully; you can sometimes hear traffic before you see it. *Note:* If your hearing isn't very sharp, looking is doubly important.   *Rule 7c*
5. The Highway Code says don't cross if there is traffic near. Therefore I should make sure there is plenty of time to walk *not* run straight across before stepping out. If not, I must find somewhere safer.   *Rule 7d & e*
6. I should keep looking and listening in case traffic suddenly comes upon me, perhaps from a side road or if the road is wider than usual and therefore takes longer to cross than a narrow one.   *Rule 7f*

 When crossing the road at night how can you make sure you are seen?

A. By wearing something reflective or bright and/or by crossing near a street lamp.   *Rules 3 & 24*

Extra Rules for Crossing at Specific Places
(See diagram on page 16)

Q How should you cross when there's an island in the road?

A. I should cross to the island using the Green Cross Code, stop there, then cross the other half of the road separately.

Rule 8

Q When crossing at a junction, what should you be especially careful about?

A. When crossing from the entrance lane side of a junction, traffic will come into the road from behind me.

Rule 9

Q Where is it dangerous to cross in the vicinity of a Zebra crossing?

A. On or near the zig-zag approach lines.   *Rule 10*

Q How do you, as a pedestrian, claim priority on a Zebra crossing? Underline one. 1. Look up and down the road. 2. Place a foot on the crossing. 3. Stand near the kerb. 4. Lie down on the pavement.

A. 2. However, I should look both ways first so that I give drivers a chance to see me and begin to slow down before I get too close. This is particularly important when it is raining, icy or at night, as startling a driver into stopping suddenly could result in an accident.   *Rule 11*

Q How should you treat a Zebra crossing if there is an island in the middle?

A. I should treat it as two separate crossings.   *Rule 13*

FACT: *The law demands that pedestrians must not loiter on any type of crossing. If you extend this to mean, don't hang around the pavement area of a crossing either, you will save much frustration to drivers who are trying to decide whether or not to slow down and stop for you.*

Q What is the significance of a Pelican crossing?

A. Pedestrians can stop the traffic by pressing a button and changing the signal in a set of traffic governing lights. *Rule 14*

Q   Once the lights have changed, you will get a special signal like these and often an audible one as well. Write below each signal what it means and indicate with a tick when the bleeping noise should sound.

1      2      3

A. 1. Wait. 2. Cross with care. 3. Do not start to cross.
Rule 14

Q   What does the flashing green man mean at a Pelican crossing?

A. Firstly, it means that if I am approaching the crossing I shouldn't start to cross. Secondly, if I am already on the crossing I can safely carry on as a few seconds are left before the lights change.   *Rule 14*

Q   How many types of Pelican crossing are there?

A. Two. One which goes straight across the road (including any central refuge) and a staggered crossing which should be treated as two separate crossings (see Rule 15 and diagram on page 7).

Q   What should you look out for when crossing at traffic lights?

A. Any pedestrian signals, which I must obey. Otherwise I should observe the state of the lights and the traffic and need to watch out for cars which may "jump" the lights. I must look out for traffic turning the corner and lights, such as green filter lights, which allow some traffic lanes to move when others are stopped.   *Rule 17*

Q When crossing where there is a policeman, traffic warden or school patrol directing, which statement is true? 1. Cross when you like. 2. Wait until there is a large group before crossing. 3. Cross when signalled to do so and pass in front of the controller.

A. Statement 3 is true.   *Rule 18*

FACT: *Guard rails are very expensive to erect and are only positioned with very good reason. They are found where pedestrians are most vulnerable, for example, on large bends, near crossings, at traffic lights and junctions and in shopping areas where your attention may be drawn away from the kerb edge, or for a few seconds, your children. Resist the urge to jump over them as if you've just won a Wimbledon final. Walk on the pavement side, not between the guard rail and the road, and find a gap in the barrier before crossing.*   *Rule 19*

 Q How should you cross a one way street?

A. I should use the Green Cross Code and wait until I could cross all the lanes (usually two or three) in one go.
                                                                  Rule 21

Q What important points should you bear in mind when crossing bus and cycle lanes?

A. First, there is an extra lane to cross. Second, unimpeded buses may travel faster than other traffic. Third, buses may actually be travelling against the flow of traffic in a contraflow bus lane. Fourth, cyclists may also use the lane.
                                                                  Rule 22

 Q Why is it dangerous to cross near or between parked vehicles?

A. Because I reduce the chance that a driver will see me. If I cross between cars, one of which has its engine running, or is about to start up (perhaps in gear), I could be crushed between them.   *Rule 23*

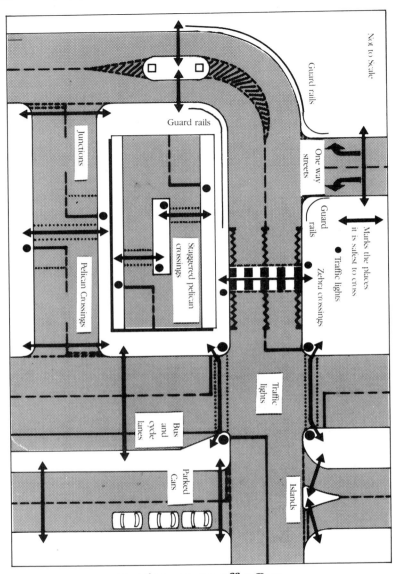

Getting on or off a Bus

Q What should you do when you want to get off a bus? 1. Jump off opposite your destination. 2. Wait until the bus slows down. 3. Wait until the bus stops at traffic lights. 4. Wait until the bus stops at a bus stop.

A. 4.

Rule 26

Q How do you call a bus at a request stop?

> *A.* I should give a clear signal. Put my arm up in plenty of time so that the driver sees me. The driver needs to look around, use his mirrors, signal, brake and make allowances for other traffic on the road before stopping for me. A late signal could make him react too quickly and cause an accident.

Q You've just got off the bus but you want to cross the road. What do you do next?

> *A.* Wait until the bus moves off again so that I have a clear view of the road before crossing. I would never cross behind or in front of the bus as I am hidden from the bus driver and from car drivers overtaking the bus. *Rule 26*

3
*T*he Cyclist

FACT: *Cyclists, you are responsible for the condition of your cycle. It should be the correct size, have efficient brakes and gears, a saddle adjusted to the correct height, a reflector and correctly inflated tyres, without bulges or holes. In this respect, follow the manufacturer's recommendations for tyre pressure. If you have a bell, use it to warn others when necessary. The chain should be lubricated and correctly tensioned. During the hours of darkness you should show a lamp at the front and rear.* Rules 187, 188, 189

 Q What is the first thing you would do before moving off, pulling in, turning left or right, passing parked cars or negotiating a roundabout?

> *A.* Look around to keep myself safe from other moving vehicles. I would also give a clear arm signal if this would help other road users.
> *Rules 126, 193, 198, 200, 201, 202 (Roundabouts).*

 Q Why should you not ride in the gutter?

A. If I were to run over a deep pothole or drain cover, I might swerve or be thrown from the bike into the path of another vehicle. I should watch out for such obstructions well ahead.

Rules 194, 195

Q Strictly speaking is it alright to ride two abreast? 1. Yes. 2. No. 3. Only on a narrow road.

A. 1. Yes, if the road is wide enough. If the road is narrow or busy I would ride in single file, a safe distance from the kerb. *Rule 209*

Q What particular danger is there in cycling when viewed from a car?

A. I have a narrow profile and can be easily overlooked by drivers, particularly when hidden by pedestrians at the kerb edge. I also move more slowly than the average road user and judging my speed may be more difficult than that of a car. *Rules 52 & 197*

Q All of these signs show cycles. Can you pair up the sign with its correct meaning? For example: sign 4 goes with meaning 1.

1.____
2.____
3.____
4.____
5.____
6.____
7.____
8.____
9.____
10.____
11.____
12.____
13.____
14.____
15.____
16.____

Meanings: 1. Lane ahead reserved for pedal cycles. 2. Advance direction sign showing different route for pedal cycles. 3. Cycle route ahead. 4. Cycle track and pedestrian path with no separation. 5. Direction to a cycle parking place (two signs). 6. No cycling. 7. Contra-flow cycle lane. 8. Recommended shared cycle/pedestrian route. 9. Separate track and path for cyles and pedestrians. 10. Route for pedal cycles only. 11. Recommended route for pedal cycles to place shown (two signs). 12. A with flow cycle lane. 13. Route recommended for pedal cycles. 14. Buses and cycles only. 15. At a pedal cycle parking place. 16. Direction sign for cycles and pedestrians.   *Rules 205 & 208*

A.   Meaning followed by sign: 1. sign 4; 2. sign 14; 3. sign 1; 4. sign 17; 5. signs 8 and 18; 6. sign 2; 7. sign 10; 8. sign 6; 9. sign 16; 10. sign 3; 11. signs 12 and 13; 12. sign 9; 13. sign 11; 14. sign 5; 15. sign 15; 16. sign 7.   *Rule 192*

 What is a cycle lane? 1. A cyclist's obstacle course. 2. An area of road on the left reserved for cyclists only. 3. A pavement area. 4. A gully which stops your wheels turning.

A.   2. My lane will have a white line boundary either solid or broken and will be on the left. I may have to share it with buses or pedestrians, but signs will tell me about this well in advance.   *Rules 203, 206, 207*

 What should cyclists wising to turn right on a busy road at night do? 1. Move out to the right of the lane. 2. Stay in the middle of the lane. 3. Keep well to the left of the lane.

A.   3. Keep over to the left and wait until the traffic has gone or a suitable gap appears for them to cross.

Rule 198

FACT: *The Highway Code gives several commonsense rules for cyclists to observe when riding along the road. Keep your hands on the handlebars and both feet on the pedals except when signalling or stopping. Carry passengers only if you have a special seat. Don't ride close behind or hold onto another vehicle. Ride in single file on cycle tracks and lanes and on narrow roads where there is traffic. Don't carry anything that will affect your balance, but if you must carry loads, keep them* *to a minimum and stow them in a basket or on a rack. Don't wear or carry any loose articles or clothing (Rule 190) which can become trapped in the wheel or chain.* Rule 209

FACT: The Law demands: *That pedal cyclists also observe traffic light signals, road signs and markings, Stop signs, the Zebra and Pelican crossing rules and traffic controllers such as school patrols and the police. Your lights must be working and be on at night. You are breaking the law if you ride recklessly, are under the influence of drink or drugs, ride on the pavement or leave it in a dangerous position.* Cycle security: *Carry a strong, well designed lock, so that you can quickly secure your cycle before leaving it.* Rules 191, 196, 199, 211

4

The Driver's Responsibilities

Your responsibilities as a driver are many, varied and most of them will cost you money. Most of the points which follow are covered in "The Road User and the Law" (The Highway Code, October 1992) A: To Drivers of Motor Vehicles [pages 67-70]).

 What do you need to display on your vehicle before driving it on the road? 1. Your photograph. 2. L plates. 3. A road fund licence.

A. 3. It is an offence not to display my road fund licence (tax disc) even if my car is only parked by the road and is not used.

 What documents must you also possess before driving?

A. My driving licence, a current test certificate (MOT) if the vehicle is over three years old and a certificate of motor insurance that covers my use of the vehicle.

Q Where may you acquire or renew your road fund licence?

A. Either from the DVLC at Swansea or a local post office.

Q What other document do you need updated if you have taken possession of a vehicle?

A. The relevant section of the registration document must be filled in and sent to DVLC in Swansea to have my name placed on it as the new registered keeper.

Q How do you know if your driving licence covers the type of vehicle you intend to drive?

A. The classes of vehicle are grouped as A, B, C, D, etc. My entitlement will be printed on the licence.

Q What makes your driving licence valid?

A. If the time I drive is within the date of issue and the date of expiry, and the licence is signed with my usual signature, in ink.

Q What types of insurance policy cover are available for your vehicle?

A. 1. Third party. 2. Third party, fire and theft. 3. Comprehensive cover.

Q What does 'third party' mean?

A. The ability of another road user to claim against my negligence should any accident occur, in order to cover their own loss by injury or damage.

Q   What does 'comprehensive cover' mean?

A. It means that as well as claims by a third party, I may also normally claim for damage to my own vehicle.

TIP: *Ask your insurance broker for a full explanation of the types of policy before paying any premiums and buying insurance cover.*

Q   What is a current test certificate and how long do they last?

A. It is a piece of paper more often called an MOT (Ministry of Transport) certificate. Some garages are authorised to test vehicles for this purpose and display a sign to that effect. A pass or failure sheet is issued depending on the result of the checks made. This will have the date of testing and the garage's identification stamp. A pass certificate expires after one year.

Q   What happens if the vehicle fails the MOT test?

A. I must decide whether it is worth having the repair done and, if so, I can do it myself or authorise the garage to repair it for a fee. Once the vehicle is repaired a pass will be issued and I can drive the vehicle again.

Q   It is your responsibility to keep your vehicle in a good roadworthy condition. What parts do you think need particular attention?

A. Lights, brakes, steering, tyres (including spare), exhaust system, seat belts, demisters, windscreen wipers and washers.   *Rule 28*

Q   Which parts of your vehicle need regular cleaning?

A. The windscreen, windows, lights, direction indicators, reflectors, mirrors, number plates and L plates (where fitted).   Rule 28

Q Must you wear glasses for driving if you wear them normally?

A. Yes, of course, because it is an offence to drive with uncorrected defective vision. *Rule 34*

FACT: *You must always be able to read a number plate from a distance of 20.5 metres (67 ft) (Rule 34). If you can't, it is your responsibility to have your eyes checked and spectacles prescribed.*

 Q You must report to the licensing authority any health condition likely to affect your driving. True or false?

A. True (See Chapter 49 on disabled drivers).

Q What are the requirements about carrying loads on your vehicle or trailer and the number of passengers you are allowed to carry?

A. 1. I must not overload my vehicle or the trailer. 2. Any load must be evenly distributed, to spread the load. 3. The load must be securely tied down if carried outside my vehicle. 4. I must not overload my vehicle with passengers to the extent that they cramp my driving area or cause danger. 5. The load must not project sideways or to the front or rear far enough to be illegal.

Q What are the rules about brakes and steering?

A. They must be correctly adjusted, efficient and in good working order.

Q What are the requirements for tyres, including the spare?

A. 1. They must be suitable for the vehicle I am driving. 2. I must check regularly that they are properly inflated to the correct pressures. 3. There must be at least 1mm of tread depth across the whole width of the tyre and around the whole circumference. 4. They must be free of cuts, embedded articles, bulges and other defects.

NOTE: *From 1 January 1992, minimum tyre tread depth was increased from 1mm to 1.6mm for cars, light vans and any towed trailer. The new law covers the central three quarters of tread width on a tyre, which must have at least 1.6mm of tread depth around the whole circumference.*

 What are the requirements for mixing (or not mixing) radial and crossply tyres?

A. It is best not to mix either type and fit all four wheels with the same tyres. I must never mix crossply and radialply tyres on the same axle. It is dangerous to place radialply on the front and crossply on the rear. Even radialply on the rear and crossply on the front isn't safe for performance cars.

 What should you remember about your windscreen, windows, windscreen wipers and washers?

A. The windscreen and other windows must be kept clean. I must periodically check that my windscreen wiper blades aren't perished and replace them as necessary. The washer bottle will need topping up and checking regularly so that I can quickly remove thrown up spray and dirt. *Rule 28*

TIP: *Don't cover your windows with stickers. Windows are for looking out of, they aren't meant to be advertising space.*

TIP: *Never use your windscreen wipers on a dry screen. Any dirt or grit will scratch the windscreen causing expensive damage. You may not notice it by day, but another car's headlights or streetlights will cause glare and spectral distractions.*

 What do you do about a frayed seat belt?

A. Get it replaced. It isn't safe to cut it and sew it myself. It is my responsiblity, as a driver, to check that the seat belts, anchorage fastenings and adjusting devices are free from defects, both for myself and my passenger. See *The Road User and The Law:* A)3) Wearing of Seat Belts, and *Rule 40*

Q How many mirrors must be fitted to your car and how should they be adjusted? 1. Lots. 2. Enough to afford a good view. 3. One interior mirror.

A. 2. It's no good if they all point down or up. My mirrors must be positioned so that I have a good view of traffic behind me, and to the sides.

Q Your horn must be in working order before driving. True or false?

A. True. I must always be able to warn others of my presence.

Q Is a broken speedometer an excuse for breaking the speed limit?

A. No. It is an offence to drive if the speedometer isn't working.

Q What is meant by an efficient exhaust system?

A. I must make sure there are no holes in the exhaust, so that it doesn't 'blow'. All the connections must be secure and airtight. All of the exhaust fumes and noise must be channelled through the silencer boxes, which must not be unsuitable or defective.

Q What is the danger of a defective exhaust system?

A. The fumes may be drawn into the vehicle and cause drowsiness.

Q What points are relevant about seating position when driving?

A. I must be able to exercise proper control over my vehicle by reaching all of the hand and mirror controls easily, and not stretching to reach foot controls. I need to retain an unobstructed view of the road and traffic ahead.

Q How must you conduct yourself when driving?

A. It is an offence to endanger other members of the public by my driving, so I must not drive recklessly. Instead I must drive with all due care and attention, showing consideration to others.

Q If your engine is somewhat worn, how many pints of oil are you allowed to burn over a given time? 1. One pint per week. 2. One litre per week. 3. 500ml per week.

A. None of these. It is an offence to drive a vehicle which emits excessive amounts of smoke and fumes.

Q What must you do before you leave your vehicle, even for a short time?

A. I must set the handbrake and switch off the engine.
Rule 137

Q When you leave your vehicle at night, or in bad daytime visibility, what else must you switch off, and what must you leave on?

A. I must ensure that my headlamps are switched off when parked and leave my sidelights on if unlit parking isn't allowed.
Rule 143

Q You have been pulled in by the police and asked to produce your documents. You tell the officer that you don't have them with you. What can the officer require that you do next? 1. Report with them to the local police station within 24 hours. 2. Show them at any police station of your choice within seven days. 3. Take them to the nearest police station within three days.

A. 2.

NOTE: *The officer, who need only have reasonable cause, can ask you to produce your driver's licence, a certificate of insurance and an MOT test certificate.* **Rule 78**

Q Is it an offence to open your vehicle door without looking around first?

A. It is if I cause injury or danger to cyclists, pedestrians or other road vehicles. I would always check first to avoid such an incident occurring. Rule 137

Q Name the requirements you need to comply with when in possession of a provisional licence and wishing to drive a car.

A. I must at all times be accompanied by a person who holds a full, valid driving licence which covers the same group of vehicle and display regulation L plates. I also need insurance to cover my use of the vehicle.

NOTE: *From October 1990, new regulations came into force which require that fully qualified drivers who wish to accompany a learner must be at least 21 years old and have held a full licence for 3 years.*
As a learner driver, it is your responsibility to ensure that the person accompanying you, while you are driving, is covered by these new regulations. Failure to do so could render you liable to a fine of up to £400 and two penalty points or discretionary disqualification. Your accompanying driver may also be liable to these penalties because of the laws regarding aiding and abetting. Please check first that you satisfy these new requirements. **Rule 36**

Q L plates must be displayed where and for how long? 1. In the windows. 2. To the front and rear. 3. On the bumpers. (a) Until you pass your test. (b) For one month after passing your test. (c) For one year whether or not you have passed your test.

A. 2 and (a). *Rule 38*

Q When you have passed your test, L plates should be: 1. Cut up into tiny pieces? 2. Given to a friend? 3. Removed from the car?

A. 3.

Q You are teaching your friend, spouse, son or daughter to drive. What do you do with the L plates when they aren't driving?

A. I should remove them from the vehicle or cover them up. *Rule 38*

5

Seat Belts

Q The Highway Code says that wearing seat belts: 1. Reduces accidents? 2. Causes less damage in accidents? 3. Halves the risk of death or serious injury? 4. Stops you escaping quickly from a damaged car?

A. 3. Rule 40

Q Who has to wear a seat belt?

A. All drivers and front or rear seat passengers (unless exempt). *Rule 40*

Q It is the driver's responsibility to ensure that child passengers know how to use, and wear their seat belts. True or false?

A. True. (Adult passengers are responsible for themselves.)

Q Who is exempt from wearing front seat belts? Underline any you think are correct. 1. Holders of a medical exemption certificate. 2. Drivers who are reversing.

3. People in a hurry. 4. Disabled drivers. 5. Drivers of delivery vans. 6. Drivers on short trips to school or the shops.

A. 1, 2 and 5. (You may have underlined 4 also, but disabled drivers need to apply for an exemption certificate from their doctor first.)

The Road User & the Law A)3) Wearing of seat belts

NOTE: *Since 1986 car manufacturers have been required by law to fit rear seat belts or child restraints as standard. Shortly afterwards (1989) drivers also became responsible for children under 14 to be restrained by these rear seat belts also, when sitting in the back.*

From 1 July 1991, this law has been extended to include adults *who are sitting in the back.*

 Where are children safest?

A. In the rear seat, properly restrained with approved devices, and, where fitted, the rear door child locks switched so that the doors cannot be opened from inside.

Rule 42

FACT: *The most important points to bear in mind when choosing rear child restraints or seat belts is that they are approved and are appropriate to size and age. Children are much safer in the back if restrained properly.*

 What is the age limit for travelling in the front?1. No limit. 2. One year old. 3. Four years old.

A. 1. There is no limit, but children under one must wear an approved child restraint designed for their age and weight.

Rule 41

Q Match up the child restraint to the most appropriate age.
1. Carry cot with special securing straps.
2. Child bucket safety seat.   Infants under 1 year.
3. Seat belt and special booster   Children aged 1, 2 or
   cushion.   3 years.
4. Rearward facing safety seat.   Children from 4 to 14
5. Safety harness.   years.

A. Infants under 1 year = 1 and 4. Children aged 1, 2 or 3 years = 2. Children from 4 to 14 years = 3 & 5. *Rule 41*

Q When there are no restraints in the rear, where are children safest?

A. In the front passenger seat, wearing an approved seat belt and booster cushion.

Q Where should children *not* be carried in an estate or hatchback car?

A. In the luggage space behind the rear seats unless proper seats are provided by the manufacturer. Kneeling up, lying down or sitting unrestrained is a dangerous way to travel.   *Rule 42*

SUMMARY: *There is really no excuse for children not to be properly restrained in the back. If you are involved in an accident, there is every probability that you will be able to unbuckle and walk away from it. Not so any unrestrained children who could come forward to the windscreen. For the sake of a few pounds and your children's lives, afford them the same protection you give yourself.*

6

Moving off

Every time you get into a car, whether it is yours or someone else's, you must perform what we call the 'cockpit drill'. This consists of a few simple checks to make sure that you are in a safe, comfortable position and can reach all of the controls easily.

 These checks consist of your driving seat, your mirror, the doors and seat belt. Can you place them in a logical sequence so that each only needs checking once?

A. DOOR — It is my responsibility to make sure that all the doors are shut, particularly when carrying children.

SEAT — Move the seat far enough forward so that I can reach all of the pedals without stretching.

SEAT BELT — This should not be twisted over me. Buckling up after adjusting the seat is easier.

MIRROR — I should adjust my mirror for a good view out of the back window. I shouldn't lean forward to look in the mirror, because when I sit back again the adjustment will be 'out'.

Q Two checks are now needed before you actually start the engine, what are they? 1. Handbrake and clutch. 2. Handbrake and neutral. 3. Neutral and footbrake?

A. 2. I must check that my handbrake is on and the gear lever in neutral.

Q Before moving off you must check your 'blind spots'. Where are they and what are they? 1. At the front of the car 2. Under the car. 3. Behind the car.

A. 3.. All cars have 'blind spots' despite the number of mirrors fitted. They are areas hidden from view along the sides and to the rear of the car.

See Rule 129 ref. REVERSING

Q When checking blind spots, what are you looking for?

A. Pedestrians, cyclists, motorcyclists, animals and other vehicles. To check my blind spot I must actually look behind and to the side of my car and not rely solely on mirrors.

Q Which of the following constitutes the correct moving off procedure? 1. Mirror, blind spot, mirror, signal if necessary, release handbrake, move off if clear and safe. 2. Mirror, signal if necessary, move off if clear, blind spot, release handbrake. 3. Release handbrake, signal , blind spot, mirror, mirror, move of if clear and safe.

A. 1 is the correct procedure. *Rule 48*

Q If you are very short and have difficulty seeing over the steering wheel, what should you do? 1. Buy a smaller car with taller seats. 2. Sit more upright. 3. Sit on a cushion.

A. 3.

Q How should your seat be positioned before driving?

A. I need to be able to reach the pedals easily and have my legs slightly bent so that when I push on the clutch, for example, I am not stretching.

Q What does proper use of the mirror mean? 1. Check it every 300 yards. 2. Looking and acting on what you see. 3. Glancing before signalling.

A. 2. Checking my mirror is a waste of time if I don't take any notice of, and act on, what I see. *Rule 51*

Q Exterior, door or wing mounted mirrors should be: 1. Properly adjusted and used regularly? 2. Properly adjusted in case they are needed? 3. Folded inwards in case they get hit?

A. 1.

FACT: *Exterior door and wing mirrors properly adjusted largely overcome blind spots to the rear, but not completely, so it is still important to look over your shoulder before moving away from the kerb.*

7

Driving along

Q Which of these cars has the correct driving position?

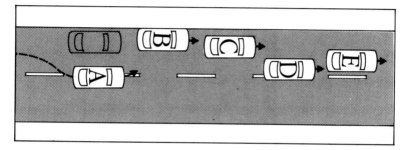

A. Cars A & C.

Q When driving along normally, what part of the road should you be on? 1. On the right. 2. On the left. 3. Alongside the lane markings.

A. 2.   *Rule 49*

Q Under what circumstances can you vary this position?

A. Any time signs or road markings indicate a positive instruction or give me a choice. When I intend to overtake either moving or stationary vehicles. If I want to turn right, I position the car to the right of my lane (just left of the middle of the road) or in the lane provided for right turns.
Rules 49, 96, 117

Q Where must you not drive your car? 1. On the pavement or footpath. 2. On the beach. 3. Onto common land.

A. 1.   *Rule 50*

FACT: *You must not normally drive on a pavement or footpath. However, you are allowed to drive over paved areas where the kerbs are lowered, in order to enter a petrol station, your own driveway and similar properties bordering a road. But remember, pavements are for people and PEDESTRIANS HAVE PRIORITY OVER ALL MOVING TRAFFIC, so give way to them before crossing into any area of this kind.*   *Rules 50, 84*

 How often should you check your rear-view mirror? 1. Every five minutes. 2. Whenever you change gear. 3. Regularly.

A. 3. I should check the mirror often and always before carrying out a manoeuvre or before changing speed. I am safer if I have a good working knowledge of the traffic situation behind and to the side of me.   *Rule 51*

FACT: *It isn't just a question of looking in your mirror regularly, but also acting on what you see is happening behind.*

 Even though you check your mirror regularly, when should you make an additional special point of using the mirrors?

A. Well before moving off, overtaking, turning left, turning right, slowing down or stopping. This should then be followed by a clear and definite signal of intention.
    Rule 51

TIP: *Remember the routine:* Mirrors — Signal — Manoeuvre. *Then divide manoeuvre into:* Position — Speed — Look.

 Who is most at risk from your actions if you don't keep a sharp look out? Think small and suggest why.

A. Pedal cyclists, motor cyclists and pedestrians. Pedestrians can seem completely oblivious of traffic and step out whenever they feel like it. Pedal cycles and motorcycles, when viewed head on, are much less easy to see and in some light appear to blend in with the background. If I am driving a long vehicle or towing a trailer I must remember to leave them plenty of room to the side and also make an extra allowance before pulling back in again.   *Rule 52*

Q When are pedestrians and pedal cyclists particularly at risk. 1. At night. 2. At noon. 3. At dusk.

A. 1 and 3. When unthinking walkers and riders do not take steps to make themselves visible. *Rule 56*

FACT: *You should drive more slowly in the wet, when there is a frost or fog and at night. Never brake sharply except in an emergency.* *Rule 57*

 Q You must make way for emergency vehicles when their lights are flashing and/or alarms are sounding, and, where safe, allow buses to pull out when they are indicating an intention to move off. True or false?

A. True. *Rule 76*

 Q What do these signs mean and how should they be interpreted?

A. Steep hill upwards and steep hill downwards. The gradients are shown as a percentage.

FACT: *Sometimes the signs show a ratio, such as 1:5 or 1:8. The percentages and ratios are equivalents of the same things. For example: 1:20 = 5%; 1:15 = 7%; 1:10 = 10%; 1:8 = 12%; 1:5 = 20%; 1:4 = 25%.*

 Q When moving off uphill from stationary or from a junction, what should you be careful of?

A. I must avoid getting in the way of any traffic climbing the hill.

 Q Why is entering or crossing traffic on a hill more difficult than on level ground?

A. On level ground driving speeds are more easily compared. But on a hill I must take into account the slow uphill traffic and the relatively faster downhill traffic before making any move.

FACT: *How hills affect the performance of your car compared to level ground.*

Going uphill:

1. The engine must work harder to maintain speed. 2. Brakes slow the car down quicker. 3. 'Engine braking' is more pronounced in any gear. 4. Gear changing must be quick to overcome rapid drops in speed when declutching. 5. Handbrake is a must when stopping and pulling away again, requires more coordination.

Going downhill:

1. Less work is done by engine to maintain speed. 2. Brakes are less effective and it takes longer to slow down. 3. Engine braking is only effective in low gears. High gears produce no engine braking at all. 4. Gear changing is harder because declutching makes the car increase speed between changes. 5. Relying on brakes alone to slow car down can result in overheating and 'fade'. 6. Low gears give you greater car control.

 What part of the road is meant by 'Dead ground'? 1. A dead end. 2. A blind corner. 3. Where the road dips ahead. 4. Where stubble burning smoke blows across the road.

A. 3. The road may be straight but can undulate along hilly ground. When I am going up a slight slope it may suddenly drop away and reveal traffic that I couldn't previously see.

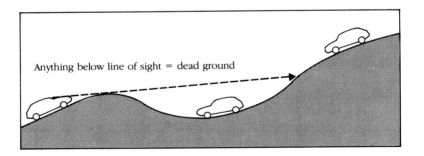

Anything below line of sight = dead ground

 How should you deal with traffic priorities on a hill? 1. Allow uphill traffic to pass freely. 2. Allow downhill traffic to pass freely. 3. Apply the same rules as you would on level ground.

A. 1. It is much more difficult to pull away again on a hill, so I would give way to traffic driving uphill, even if an obstruction was on the right side. This is particularly important if the upcoming vehicle is a heavy lorry or coach.

8

Road Junctions

FACT: *Road junctions are the places where the vast majority of accidents occur. It is important that you as a driver know how to approach, what to do, where you should be, where to look and how to emerge safely. Chapters 9 and 10, Turning Left and Turning Right, will be of benefit if you're not too sure.*

 What sort of points do you think are relevant when negotiating a junction?

A. I must approach with care and be prepared to stop. 2. Consider my position and speed. 3. I shouldn't emerge until I'm sure it's safe. 4. I should never pull out or across a road so as to block the junction. 5. When lorries are in front of me I should hang back so that the driver can use the whole width of the road to make the turn if need be. 6. I must keep a look out for pedal cyclists and motor cyclists on my left, and also approaching from the right. There may in addition be pedestrians crossing around the junction area. *Rule 107*

 When waiting at a junction, you notice the vehicle coming toward you from the right is signalling its intention to turn left. What do you do? 1. Pull out, only if you want to turn left. 2. Pull halfway across the road and wait for traffic from the left to clear before turning right. 3. Wait until the car actually turns off before pulling out.

A. 3. I should never pull out until I am sure what the vehicle is going to do; the signal may be a mistake on the part of the driver. *Rule 111*

Q Where would you be likely to see this road marking painted? What is it for?

A. On approach to a junction where I am required to 'Give Way' to other traffic on the main road. It is a warning triangle (elongated because of my angle of view to it) which is helpful in fog, mist or at night, so that I don't come upon the end of the road unexpectedly.   *Rule 110*

Q What do these signs mean and where would you be more likely to see sign 2?

1   2

A. Sign 1 — is a Give Way sign found at junctions where I must give priority to traffic on the other road which is crossing in front of me. Sign 2 means the same but is more likely to occur where there are Give Way lines after a bend, or where faster open road traffic will shortly have to slow down to negotiate a junction.   *Rule 110*

Q What road marking will indicate that the junction ahead is a Give Way junction? 1. A solid white line. 2. Double broken white lines. 3. A single broken white line.

A. 2.   *Rule 110*

Q Give Way lines at the end of a one way street are: 1. Marked across all of the lanes? 2. There are no markings except at traffic lights? 3. Short diagonal stripes?

A. 1.

Q What do these signs mean and where would you be more likely to see sign 2?

1   2

A. Sign 1 means that I must stop at the junction and wait for a safe gap in the traffic before moving off. Sign 2 is an advance warning sign of a Stop junction, perhaps at the bottom of a hill or before a bend.   *Rule 109*

 Q What road markings will you see at a junction where you must stop? 1. A solid white line across your lane. 2. A zig-zag line across your lane. 3. A broken line across the whole junction.

A. 1.   *Rule 109*

 Q How would you cross or turn right into a dual-carriageway? 1. Treat each half as a separate road. 2. Cross all of the dual-carriageway in one movement. 3. Both 1 and 2 when appropriate.

A. 3. If there is a central reservation wide enough to take my vehicle, I would cross to there first, and then negotiate the second half. If not, I should wait in the side road until I can cross all of the dual-carriageway in one go.   *Rule 112*

 Q The vehicle in front has halted at a Stop line, the road seems very clear, the driver pulls away, what do you do?

A. I drive up to the solid line and stop. Just because the road was clear for the leading car, it doesn't follow that I am also safe. I check for myself that it is safe to pull out. *Rule 109*

NOTE: *If a policeman is controlling traffic at a Stop line and beckons your lane forward, it is not necessary to stop at the line.*

FACT: *When there are long vehicles turning at a junction, be extra careful. For example, if a lorry is in the right lane with its left indicator on, don't assume the driver has made a mistake and pull up alongside. If the driver hasn't seen you he may run over your car with the rear wheels as the trailer cuts the corner.*

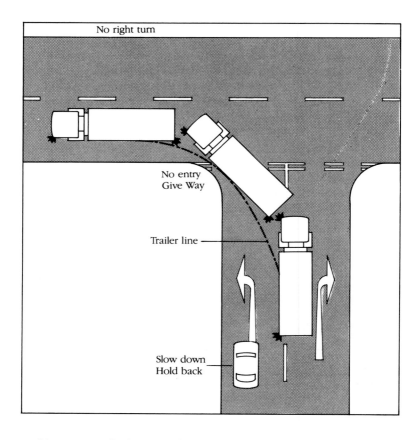

Turning right for the lorry isn't such a big problem because there is an extra bit of road to use (the width of one lane extra). Nevertheless, the driver may need to keep well over to the left before turning, so again hang back if you're turning right.

Rule 107

Q   If you were coming up behind this row of stationary cars waiting at traffic lights where would you stop to wait and why? Draw in your car.

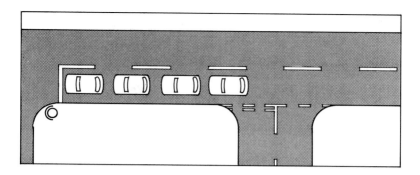

A. I would stop behind the junction so that I don't block the path of other vehicles turning right, whether into or out of the side road.

Rule 107

Q Draw in the road markings (words, lines and signs) that you would likely find at these two junctions.

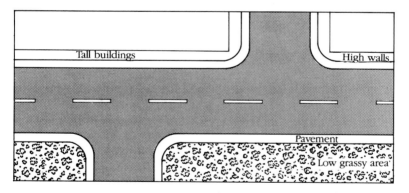

Tall buildings

High walls

Pavement

Low grassy area

A. The junction at the top would likely have a Stop sign and a solid white line at the exit because of the wall and buildings. The word STOP is painted on the road. The lines would look like this:

The junction at the bottom is fairly open and so would likely be a Give Way junction. The lines would look like this:

41

Q What does the Highway Code recommend should be a driver's system of approach to all hazards, including junctions? 1. Mirror, signal, manoeuvre. 2. Signal, mirror, manoeuvre. 3. Mirror, manoeuvre, signal.

A. 1.

NOTE: *The manoeuvre should then be broken down into position, speed and look as in Turning Left and Turning Right.*
Rules 51, 99, 117

9
Turning Left

Q You want to turn left at the next junction. Describe the general sequence you would use to make the turn safely.

A. I would use my mirrors, then give a left turn signal. After checking for cyclists on the left and allowing free passage to any pedestrians crossing, I'd make the turn without swinging out to the right before or after the turn.
Rule 108

Points in order for turning in.
Course: Decide on the direction you are going (left).
Mirror: Check on the traffic situation behind.
Signal: Indicate your intended course in plenty of time.
Position: Don't alter your road position unnecessarily, keep your normal driving position.
Brake: Slow the car down to a safe speed.
Gear: Select an appropriate gear for the turn and your speed (most often second gear).
Observation: Look up the road to check that no one has a right turn signal on and may cut across in front of you. Look into the sideroad for pedestrians crossing and cars parked around the corner. Check your nearside mirror for cyclists or motor cyclists coming up on your inside. Look around again.
Steer: Drive around the corner keeping as close in as safety allows without swinging out as indicated by the red dotted lines. Check around parked cars before moving out and don't

include them in the curve of your turn.

Mirror: Once in the new road, check your interior mirror again so that you know if anybody follows you in.

Rule 121

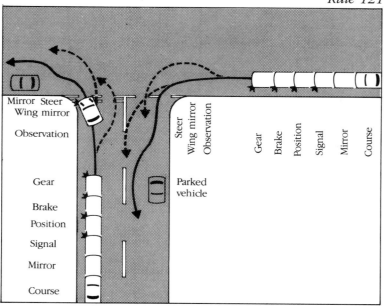

Mirror Steer
Wing mirror
Observation

Gear
Brake
Position
Signal
Mirror
Course

Steer
Wing mirror
Observation

Parked
vehicle

Gear
Brake
Position
Signal
Mirror
Course

Points in order for entering or emerging from a side road.

Points for emerging.

Course: Decide on the direction you are going (left).

Mirror: Check on the traffic situation behind.

Signal: Indicate your intended course in plenty of time.

Position: Stay in your normal driving position unless there is a left lane for you to use.

Brake: Slow the car down to a safe speed.

Gear: Select an appropriate gear for the turn and your speed (usually second gear).

Observation: At least 20 yards from the junction look right, left, right. Also check your nearside mirror for cyclists and motor cycles. If you have slowed the car down sufficiently you should have time to look right, left, right again. Because you have started looking early enough you ought to be able to decide whether the road is clear enough for you to pull out BEFORE you get to the junction (assuming an unobstructed view). If so — keep going in second gear. If not — stop at the Give Way lines and select first gear, while looking for a safe gap.

Steering: Just as you get up to the lines start to steer left so that you use the natural camber of the road to go around the corner. This reduces the chance of swinging out into the other lane. If you need to stop, your wheels are already pointing left for when you pull away again. Don't include parked vehicles in the curve of your turn, check up the main road for oncoming traffic before moving out from behind them.

Mirror: Finally check your interior mirror once again just in case traffic is coming up behind quicker than you think.

Rule 121

 Who is at most risk as you make a left turn and why? 1. You. 2. Your car. 3. Pedal and motor cyclists. 4. Lorries.

A. 3. Cyclists are in danger because they usually come up on the left hand side. If they are alongside my car when I signal there is every chance they haven't noticed it.

Rules 107 & 121

 Before turning left across a bus lane, what should you do?

A. Look to see if there are any buses or cyclists using the lane. My mirrors may not be enough so I would check my blind spot. *Rule 122*

 When turning a left corner or driving around a left bend, your speed should be at its lowest. 1. 20 yards before the bend? 2. At the start of the bend? 3. One third of the way round the bend?

A. 2. Just as I start to turn the bend or corner my car should be under acceleration, with the engine just pulling.

NOTE: *This is to drive the car around the corner and so avoid the 'floating' feeling of a car out of control. It does not mean heavy acceleration and a rapid increase in speed. Save that for after you have negotiated the bend.*

 What position do you use to negotiate a left bend and why? 1. Well to the left. 2. Offside wheels level with the centre line.

A. 1. I would keep well to the left and slow down because my view is restricted. This will keep me out of the path of anyone coming from the other direction who may be cutting the corner along the centre line.

Left bends. It is important to slow down before the bend. Your view is restricted (dotted lines) and you may come upon pedestrians, animals or a breakdown. Compare this with the view when coming the other way. Car B can see much further ahead than Car A.

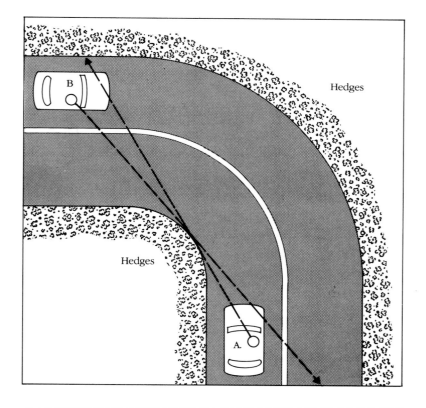

Q You are on approach to a sharp bend and realise that you are travelling too fast to negotiate it safely. What should you do? 1. It should never happen. 2. Brake gently all the way round the bend. 3. Brake firmly before the bend. 4. Brake after and stop to calm down.

A. 3 is correct, but if I am reading the road ahead properly 1 would be the more likely answer.

45

Q What do these three signs mean? 1. Turn left ahead. Turn left. Keep left. 2. Keep left. Turn left. Turn left ahead. 3. Keep left. Turn left ahead. Turn left.

 1  2  3

A. 1. Turn left. 2. Turn left ahead. 3. Keep left.

Q What does this sign mean?

A. No left turn.

Q What is the difference between these two signs and what do they both mean?

1 2

A. 1. Sharp deviation of route to left (or right if chevrons are reversed). 2. Sharp *temporary* deviation of route to left (or right if chevrons are reversed).

Q What does this sign mean and what should you do about it?

A. The sign means double bend first to left (may be reversed). I would slow down on approach then select an appropriate gear for my speed.

10
Turning Right

The general sequence to use for turning right is, Mirrors —
Signal — Manoeuvre. This is then further broken down to
include, Position — Speed — Look. Note that turning right is
much more dangerous than turning left, because you have to
cross the path of oncoming traffic. Read through the right
turn sequence so that you are thoroughly conversant with it.

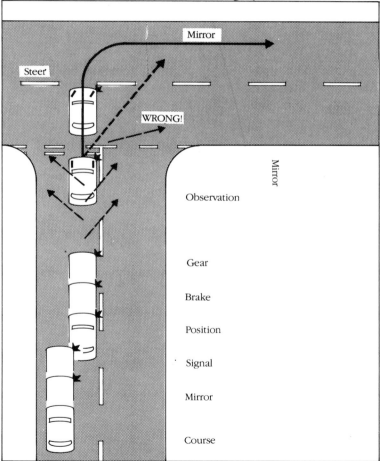

You want to turn right at the end of the road.
Course: Decide on your direction — right.

Mirror: Check on the traffic situation behind.

Signal: Indicate your intended course in plenty of time.

Position: Guide the car over to just left of the middle of the road, or the white line. If there is a lane marked for turning right, use it. If the road is wide enough, try to allow enough room for traffic to come up alongside so that other drivers can turn left, but don't put yourself at risk from traffic turning left, by moving over too far.

Brake: Slow down.

Gear: Select an appropriate gear for your speed — usually second.

Observation: At least 66 feet (20m) from the junction, start to look, right — left — right. If the junction is 'open' and clear, take a final look left and right. Keep your wheels straight and drive straight across the road, until the front of your car reaches the centre of the road you are turning into.

Steering: Steer right now so that you don't cut the corner.

Mirror: Check your mirror again in case traffic is coming up quicker than you think.

Where your view is obstructed by buildings or fences.

Observation: Where you can't see very far up the main road, still do your observation early, so that you can judge the amount of traffic. As you approach the junction, you will see more and more each time. Come down to the end of the road and stop. Take a final look right — left — right. Drive straight across in first gear, if clear.

*Steering:*Again don't cut the corner.   *Rule 117*

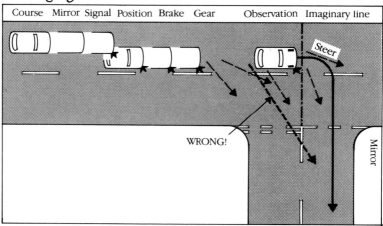

| Course | Mirror | Signal | Position | Brake | Gear | Observation | Imaginary line |

WRONG!

Steer

Mirror

You want to turn right into the side road.

Course: Decide on your direction — right.

Mirror: Check on the traffic situation behind, is anyone about to overtake you?

Signal: Indicate your intended course in plenty of time.

Position: Guide your car over to a position just left of the middle or the road or white line. Where the road is wide enough, try to allow enough room for traffic to pass on the left if you have to stop, but don't put yourself at risk from oncoming traffic by moving over too far.

Brake: Slow down to a speed suitable for the turn.

Gear: Select an appropriate gear for the turn and your speed — usually second.

Observation: Look into the side road as far as possible, and along the opposite lane for oncoming traffic. Look further into the side road for pedestrians crossing, parked cars, cars waiting to emerge right. Give way to any oncoming traffic and allow any pedestrian to cross the side road.

Steeering: By now your car will be level with the turn, but where do you start steering? Look for the centre white line in the side road and imagine it extended across your road. Keep your wheels straight until then. Turn now, so you don't cut the corner.

Mirror: Check your mirror again in the side road to see who follows you in.

When you are prevented from turning by oncoming traffic, wait at the position level with your imaginary line, your wheels straight. Look for a gap in oncoming traffic. When you see one, check all your mirrors in preparation, because, by now, traffic could be passing on your left, and someone may try to overtake you on the right (crazy, I know, but it occasionally happens anyway). By this time, the safe gap will be approaching and you can drive around in first gear.

Rule 117

 When taking up your road position for turning right, what thoughts should you have about blocking the road?

A. If I am behind a queue of traffic turning right and we are all just left of the white line, am I blocking the advance of traffic turning left into the side road because of parked vehicles on my right?

 When turning right out of a narrow side road, which is only just wide enough to allow one lane of traffic in each

direction, where should you position your vehicle?
1. Well to the left. 2. One foot from the white centre line.
3. On the right.

A. 1. Because I must also think about vehicles wanting to turn in. Of course, when turning right from a narrow road into a side road, I would also keep over to the left, while I give way to oncoming traffic.

Q Do you know what these signs mean? 1. No reversing/ No right turn/No U turns. 2. No right turns/No left turns/ No looking right. 3. Turn right ahead/Bend to right/ Keep right.

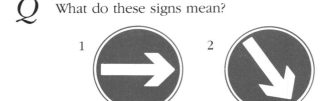

A. 1. No U turns. 2. No right turns. 3. Bend to right.

Q What do these signs mean?

A. 1. Turn right. 2. Keep right.

Q You are approaching a sharp right hand bend with tall hedges on both sides. What action should you take? Choose from the following. 1. Check your mirror. 2. Indicate right. 3. Slow down. 4. Sound horn, when necessary. 5. Keep to centre of the road. 6. Keep well over to the left. 7. Change down if necessary.

A. 1, 3, 4, 6 and 7.

Q Describe what is happening here, as if you were driving, first car A, then car B.

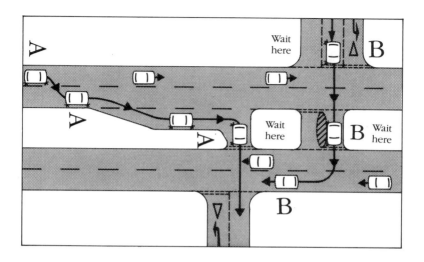

A. In car A I am turning right from a dual-carriageway into a side road. I check my mirror and signal right, then move into the right lane and the slip road. I slow down and wait in the central reservation, opposite the side road. I should be quite safe here as the islands are protecting me from traffic on both sides. While I check to cross the second half of the carriageway, I am preparing my car to move forward and then cross when safe. *Rules 117, 120*

In car B I am turning right from a side road onto the dual-carriageway. I have checked my mirror, signalled and positioned the car correctly in the right lane. When the traffic from my right has gone, I move straight across to the central reservation and wait again for the second carriageway to be clear, before driving over to the left lane. *Rule 112*

Q What happens when there is no central reservation big enough for you to wait in, when turning right?

A. I only turn right when *both* of the carriageways (to my right and left) are clear. *Rule 112*

Q You want to turn right from a one way street into a two way major road. Where should you position your vehicle? 1. In the left lane. 2. Just left of the centre white line. 3. In the right lane.

A. 3.

Q When negotiating a right hand bend, which way will the camber of the road tend to tip your car? 1. To the right. 2. To the left. 3. Forward. 4. Backward.

A. 2.

Crossroads

Q When turning right at a junction where the oncoming vehicle also wants to turn right, what vehicle position should you adopt?

A. Normally I would keep the oncoming car on my right, so that we both pass behind each other (offside to offside).
Rules 118, 119

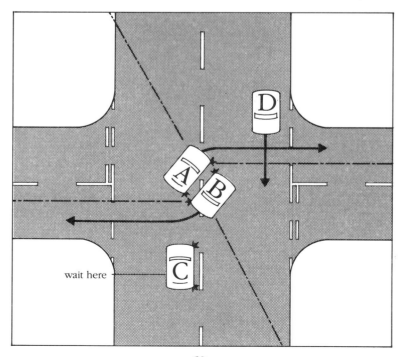

In this diagram of vehicles turning right look at the position of each car and think about what is happening. Car A has gone forward and passed car B, offside to offside, but, can't go across to the side road yet because car D has priority. Car B has pulled forward and is passing car A, offside to offside. There is no reason why it can't proceed carefully in front of car C and into the side road. Car C is correct in waiting here and not pulling forward behind car A. There is now a big enough gap to allow car B to proceed. Car D should be the only one not affected by these moves, but the driver should be careful in case car A cuts across in front.

FACT: *When passing offside to offside, as in the diagram, you are able to see clearly the road you are trying to cross and the side road you are turning into, indicated by the dotted line.*

Q Why is nearside to nearside passing, when turning right, more dangerous than offside to offside? 1. Because vehicles are closer together. 2. Because the traffic lights may change. 3. Because both drivers' views are obstructed.

A. 3.   *Rules 118, 119*

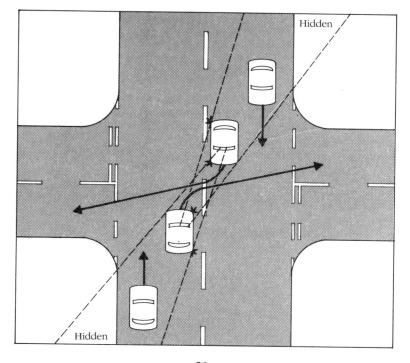

FACT: *The Highway Code says that when necessary, because of the traffic situation, the layout of the road or because the road markings indicate that you may do so, passing nearside to nearside is alright, but with one major disadvantage.*

The diagram on the previous page shows, by the dotted line, how cars which are overtaking on the left are hidden from the view of drivers trying to turn right.

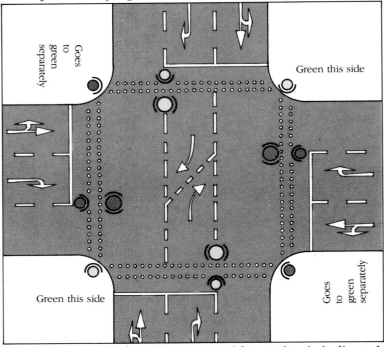

In this diagram, nearside to nearside passing is indicated when turning right. When the green lights are red, stop at the stop line. Pull forward when the lights are green and allow free passage to oncoming traffic before turning right. If the lights change back to red, move off when oncoming traffic is stopped. You have a few seconds before traffic will start coming from the left or right. Do not sit there if the lights change, because you will block the junction. At some light systems, you may also have a green filter light, which allows you to go when oncoming traffic is halted.

In order not to block the junction, when there are cars in front of you, wait at the Stop line until there is a reasonable chance of your making the move before the lights change again. The two side roads have light systems which change to green separately.

11
Traffic Light Signals

Q What is the sequence of traffic lights colours? 1. Red, amber, green, amber, red. 2. Red, amber, green, green and amber, red. 3. Red, red and amber, green, amber, red.

A. 3.
Highway Code

Q Look at these sets of traffic lights and allocate the correct meaning to each. 1. This light is telling you that you can

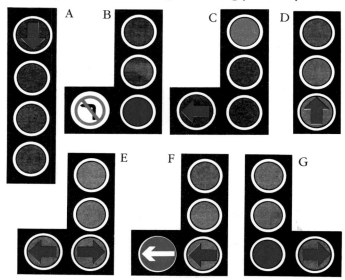

move off, but must not turn left. 2. The arrows on this light are indicating that you may not go straight on. 3. An arrow replaces the full green because traffic may only go straight on. 4. This light is telling you you go straight on only, while traffic on your right can move right. 5. This light means that you can filter left even though other traffic must stop. 6. An arrow replaces the full green because moving right or straight on is prohibited. 7. This light tells you that you can move on provided you only want to go straight on.

A. 1 — B. 2 — E. 3 — D. 4 — G. 5 — C. 6 — F. 7 — A.

Q What does it mean when the red light is showing? 1. You can keep going if you are moving too fast to stop. 2. Stop at the Stop line. 3. Move up and stop level with the lights. 4. Stop about three car lengths from the junction.

A. 2. The solid white line shows me where I should wait.

Q What does it mean when the red and amber lights come on?

A. This signal also means STOP. However, I can be fairly certain that green will follow in a few seconds. It is then, and only then, that I may drive forward.

FACT: *Some drivers call red and amber the 'get set' signal and promptly roar across the junction. This is very dangerous, especially if a driver at a side road went through on an amber light. However, there is no reason why you should not use this few seconds to prepare your car to move, so that you need only to complete your observation, when you get the green light.*

Q The green light gives you priority over other traffic. True or false?

A. True, but I have been offered priority only by the traffic light system. It is my responsibility to make sure that the junction is clear of traffic and pedestrians before moving off.

Q What does the amber light mean at traffic lights? 1. Stop at the Stop line. 2. Go, if clear. 3. Stop unless you have already crossed the Stop line. 4. Brake hard and stop. 5. Stop, unless you are so close you may cause an accident. 6. Stop just past the Stop line if necessary.

A. 1, 3 and 5 are correct.

Q You are approaching a set of lights which are showing red and amber, do you stop or just carry on?

A. If I am a reasonable distance away, I would take my foot off the accelerator and slow down because the light will change to green. If I am close I will stop. *Rule 114*

Q Some traffic lights have a green arrow pointing to the left or right, in addition to the normal lights. What is the purpose of this arrow?

A. It allows traffic to turn in the direction of the arrow, if the way ahead is clear, even if the traffic wanting to go straight on has to wait at the red light. If I want to turn left and select the correct lane in plenty of time, I can move on from the junction, leaving it free for other traffic.

Q What happens when a green arrow is pointing right? 1. The oncoming traffic will always be stopped by a red light. 2. The oncoming traffic may not be stopped by a red light. 3. You must give precedence to oncoming traffic if their lights are green and only move across in a safe gap. Two statements are true. Which two?

A. 2 and 3.

Q What is the difference between traffic signals at a junction and the type used at a Pelican crossing?

A. Junction traffic lights are changed automatically by a time switch and are all interconnected. Pelican crossing lights change only when a pedestrian starts the sequence by pressing a button. The sequential difference is Red, Red and Amber, Green, Amber, Red — junction lights. Green, Amber, Red, Flashing Amber, Green — Pelican crossings.

Q What do these two signs mean?

1 2

A. 1. Traffic signals ahead. May also be found at Pelican crossings. 2. Failure of traffic light signals. *Rule 116*

12
Junctions Controlled by Traffic Lights

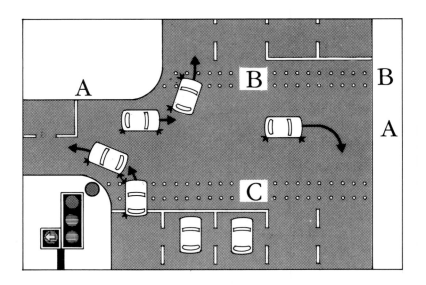

Q Look at this diagram. Imagine the road marking arrows for the lanes approaching this junction. Then decide what lights should be showing in the enlarged signal, and also for the other lights, A, B and C.

A. I have put the 'straight ahead' arrows in the right hand and middle lane, and a left turn arrow in the left lane. The lights are switched to green at A, red at B and red at C. The enlarged signal is red with an illuminated green arrow.

Q Look at this diagram. It is a traffic light controlled junction. 1. What is the rule about moving forward in this instance? 2. Draw in the shaded car and lorry again so that both of them are breaking the law. 3. Why are the cars A and B wrong in moving forward?

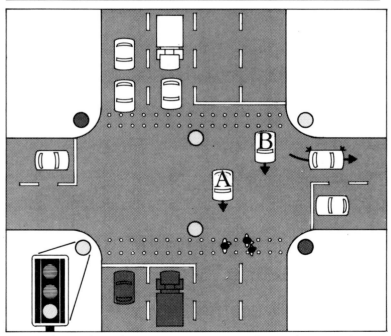

A. 1. The rule is, I must never go forward, even when I have the green light, if I cannot clear the junction safely and completely. 2. I have moved the car and lorry forward to the vehicles in front. Both are across the pedestrian lane and also blocking the junction. 3. The vehicles A and B should give way to pedestrians, but are still moving forward *Rule 114*

Q What is the rule to remember when approaching a set of traffic lights which have a green filter signal?

A. I must not get into the filter lane if I do not intend to go in the direction shown by the filter arrow. *Rule 115*

Q Where do you stop your vehicle, when required, at a traffic light?

A. I must wait behind the solid white Stop line marked across the approach to the junction. *Rule 114*

Q What special precautions should you take when you get a green light and intend turning left or right?

A. I must be especially careful of motor cyclists and pedal cyclists on either side of me, and any pedestrians that are crossing the road I am turning into. I must give them priority and plenty of room. *Rule 121*

13

Junctions Controlled by Police or Traffic Wardens

Q The lights have failed and a police officer is controlling the junction. You are in the left lane and want to filter left, but the officer is holdingup the traffic on your immediate right from going straight on, or right. Your signal is on and the junction is temporarily clear. Can you move off? 1. Yes. 2. No. 3. Yes, if the officer drops his hand. 4. Yes, if I can make it before traffic comes across from the right.

A. 2. No. I must not move forward until the officer signals me to do so. *The Highway Code*

Q Who has the authority to direct traffic on the roads? 1. A uniformed police officer. 2. Anyone. 3. A farmer. 4. A traffic warden. 5. A security guard. 6. A school crossing patrol.

A. 1, 4 and 6 (with a STOP-CHILDREN sign). It is an offence to wilfully disobey or ignore their signals.

Rule 47 & The Road User & the Law

A

B

C

D

E

F

Q Look at the pictures of the police officer directing traffic and match with statements below.

1. This officer is beckoning a vehicle from behind to move forward.

2. This officer is beckoning on vehicles from a side road.

3. This officer is ordering vehicles in front to stop.

4. This officer is telling vehicles approaching from behind to stop.

5. This officer is beckoning on a vehicle from in front.

6. This officer is ordering vehicles directly in front and behind of her to stop.

A. 1 — E. 2 — F. 3 — A. 4 — C. 5 — D. 6 — B.

Arm Signals to Persons Controlling Traffic

It helps to speed the flow of traffic if a police officer or traffic warden knows exactly where you want to go. So there is a system of arm signals you can use for this purpose, as well as your direct indicators.

NOTE: *Notice how the palm of the hand is positioned for these signals (facing forward).*

Q How would you let a police officer know you wanted to turn right?

    A. I would extend my right arm out of the window, like this:

Q How would the officer interpret these signs if you were to indicate them to him on approach to the crossroads?

A

B

    A. He would understand them as meaning 'I want to go straight on' for A, and 'I want to turn left' for B.

14

Lines and Lanes Along the Road

SUMMARY: *First, here is a summary of the road markings which you may see in front of you* across *the carriageway.*
1. Found at a road junction, these double broken lines mean give way to traffic on the major road.
2. Found at the entrance to a roundabout, this broken line means give way to traffic from the right in a roundabout.
3. Found at the entrance to a mini-roundabout, this broken line means give way to traffic from the immediate right.
4. This thick solid line, found at a junction, where your side views are seriously restricted and where there is a Stop sign, means Stop at the line.
5. A thinner solid line which, nevertheless, still means Stop. Found at traffic lights, the line means stop at the red light or police control.

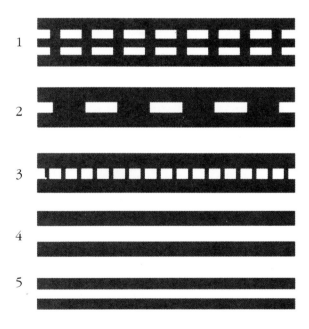

Why are there traffic lane road markings? 1. To guide you along the road. 2. To help you keep left. 3. To tell you when it is safe to overtake. 4. As an aid during bad weather. 5. So you can ignore them. 6. To warn of hazards ahead. 7. To tell you it is safe to increase speed.

A. 1, 2, 4 and 6.

Q What general rules govern the amount of paint used for lines? 1. The more paint, the safer an area. 2. The more emphatic the marking, the greater the hazard. 3. Less paint indicates a greater hazard.

A. 2.

FACT: *Nowhere will you find a sign, signal or road marking which indicates that it is safe to overtake. It is up to you to weigh up the traffic and road conditions before contemplating any overtaking manoeuvre.*

Q These lane lines are used to divide up the traffic. What is their significance?

A. 1. The short broken white lines, with long gaps, divide the road into lanes.   *Rule 87*

   2. Is a road centre line, the paint and gap being of about equal length.

   3. Is a pre-hazard warning line, notice the short gaps. Found on approach to bends, junctions and other potentially hazardous areas.   *Rule 83*

Q What does the hazard warning line mean? 1. Do not cross. 2. Do not cross unless the road is clear well ahead. 3. Cross at any time as you have priority.

A. 2.   *Rule 83*

Q What rules govern your use of the road?

A. 1. Keep left (Rule 49). 2. Keep my vehicle between the traffic lane markings (Rule 87). 3. Only move out from the left lane to overtake, pass parked vehicles, or to avoid an accident (Rule 49). 4. I can move over nearer to the middle line when I want to turn right (Rule 117). 5. I mustn't move unnecessarily from lane to lane (Rules 88 & 89). 6. I must keep a resonable distance from the kerb, but without driving along or over the centre line.

Q Sometimes, coloured reflecting road studs called 'cat's eyes' are used in conjunction with the white lines. They are coloured white, red, amber or green and shine back at you when your headlights are on at night. Where will you find each colour used?

A. White studs mark the lanes or centre of the road. Red studs mark the left hand edge of the carriageway. Amber studs mark the central reservation of dual carriageways. Green studs mark the edge of the carriageway at lay-bys and side roads.   *Rule 87*

Q What is the safest way to change lanes, when this becomes necessary?

A. First, I would use my mirrors to check on any vehicles approaching from behind. Then, if safe, signal my intention before moving over. I should avoid forcing my way into a small gap or making other vehicles swerve or slow down. 'Jumping the queue' in traffic jams is very dangerous because other drivers are not expecting me to cut in. I would be careful to avoid this at all costs.

Rules 89 & 91

NOTE: *When coming to a junction, rely on the signs and lane indication arrows to choose the lane you require for your destination. At some junctions, lanes may go in different directions. Select your lane early using the above procedure.*

Rule 90

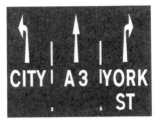

Q When there are continuous double white lines along the middle of the road, what do they mean? 1. No crossing the line nearest to you. 2. Cross only if safe. 3. Only cross to overtake.

A. 1. I must not overtake another moving vehicle if, to do so, I need to cross over or straddle the lines.   *Rule 84*

Q You are driving along and notice a vehicle parked or broken down at the road edge. However, there are also double white continuous lines before a bend. Nevertheless, you decide to overtake. Have you broken the law? 1. Yes, definitely. 2. I should wait for the police to arrive. 3. No, I can pass.

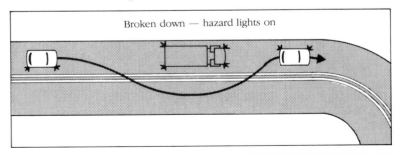

Broken down — hazard lights on

A. 3 is correct, provided I am sure it is safe to pass. Approaching traffic has priority. I can cross or straddle the line to get in or out of premises or a side road, to comply with the directions of a policeman or traffic warden, or to avoid a stationary obstruction, such as this broken down vehicle. *Rule 84*

 Q Why is there a distinction made between overtaking moving vehicles and overtaking a stationary obstruction when crossing the solid continuous centre lines?

A. Because to overtake moving vehicles needs much more road space and length of road for the manoeuvre, as well as higher speeds. Stationary obstructions are passed relatively quickly.

 Q At times there is a solid continuous white line on one side of the road, and a broken one on the other. What do the lines mean when the broken line is on your side? 1. It is safe to overtake. 2. You may overtake if safe. 3. It is not safe to overtake.

A. 2. I may cross the broken line if it is safe to do so, and if I can cross back again before reaching a solid white line on my side. *Rule 85*

 Q What indication will there be that you are approaching an area covered by a solid continuous white line on your side of the road? 1. A traffic sign. 2. Traffic signals. 3. Road arrows pointing back to the left.

A. 3.

 Q Where there are continuous solid white lines or where one line is broken, should you park? 1. Only if the broken line is on your side. 2. No, you may not park. 3. You can park anywhere in the absence of yellow lines.

A. 2 is right, but with certain provisions. I may stop briefly to load or unload goods or passengers and, meanwhile, other vehicles may cross the lines to pass me. However, I must be sensible by keeping away from bends and as far into the side as possible.

SUMMARY:

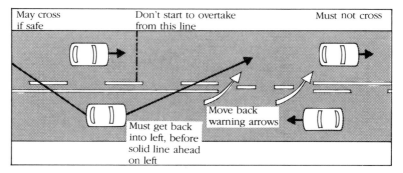

FACT: *Sometimes, because of a particularly dangerous road condition, it becomes necesssary to separate streams of opposing traffic, to protect traffic turning right, or to steer traffic away from a building close to the edge of the road. Where this occurs, white diagonal stripes or white chevrons are painted on the road.*

Q What do you do about areas which are painted like this? 1. Use it as a parking area. 2. Avoid driving onto these areas if you possibly can. 3. Drive on them to turn right.

A. 2.   *Rule 86*

Q Where a chevron area has a solid white edge line: 1. It will also have a kerb? 2. There will be traffic islands? 3. You must not enter the area except in an emergency? 4. Do not enter the area unless you want to turn right?

A. 3.   *Rule 86*

SUMMARY: *Don't cross into a striped area except in an emergency.*

A protection lane for traffic turning right. Often there are islands at the hatched areas to further safeguard the right lane traffic.

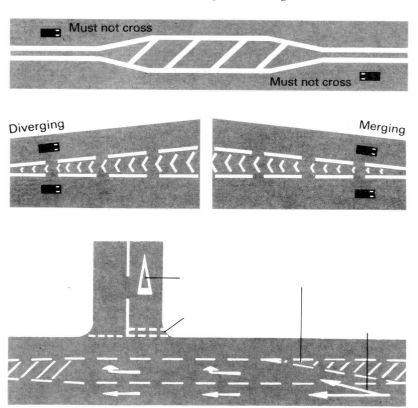

Lines are found along the left hand edge of the road as shown following.

1. On approach to junctions with Give Way lines.
2. On approach to other junctions and lay-bys.
3. To indicate the edge of main carriageway at bends and other hazards; also used on some dual carriageways.
4. Found elsewhere except on motorways.

Q Occasionally you will see black and white banded posts at the side of the road. On your left (nearside), the top portion has a red reflector, while on the right (offside), the top portion has a white reflector. What are they for?

A. They are to mark the edge of the carriageway and provide a warning to the driver. Normally they are positioned in danger areas, such as bends, at a roadside water ditch, wall, steep bank or where there is a large drop into an adjacent field.

Other worded signs on the road are as follows.

1. This SLOW sign is found near sharp bends, where to take them quickly would result in a skid or worse. Also where there are junctions just around, or on, the corner.

2. STOP on the road is displayed in conjunction with the hexagonal Stop sign.
3. NO ENTRY is written where you pass a one way street on your left or right. It is used in conjunction with no entry signs. It may be written in car parks and used without signs.

4. Where your lane is held up regularly at traffic lights or near a busy Give Way junction, if you line up alongside another side road, you will see KEEP CLEAR painted on the road. This is so that the road remains available to other traffic.

Using the Lanes

Q Which lane do you normally drive in and what are the exceptions?

A. I normally drive in the left lane. However, I may drive along the centre or to the right of the road for a short period when safe to overtake moving or parked vehicles or to turn right in a one way street.

 Q Where there are traffic islands in the road, where should they normally be when you pass them? 1. On your left. 2. On your right. 3. On either side.

A. 2. They will normally be on my right, as there is usually a 'keep left' sign placed on the bollard.

 Q What does this sign mean and where is it found? 1. Road lanes separate to different destinations, so get in lane. 2. Pass either side to reach same destination.

A. The sign is sometimes found on a traffic island where lanes are divided and means 'Vehicles may pass either side to reach same destination'. Often seen in one way streets when traffic is separated for some reason.

 Q What do you do about roads which have no lane markings, country roads or resurfaced roads for instance? 1. Divide the road into lanes with your mind's eye. 2. Use the whole of the road as your lane until another vehicle approaches. 3. Use the middle of the road if safe.

A. 1. I know what a marked lane looks like and I imagine the road divided into two.

 Q Which part of the lane do you drive in and why? 1. Well to the left. 2. On the right unless I want to turn left. 3. Slightly left of middle.

A. 3. By keeping slightly left of the middle of my driving lane, I am out of the gutter and also away from the centre line and therefore oncoming traffic (See Chapter 2 on pedestrians' safety.)

Changing Lanes

 You have changed lanes in town to pass a line of parked cars on the left. What are the main dangers here?

A. If I don't keep far enough away I can miss the indicator signal of a vehicle, which could pull out in front of me. The doors may open without warning or a pedestrian may walk out between them.

TIP: *It is up to you to drive with awareness, by trying to anticipate the actions of others (cyclists, pedestrians and other drivers). It is inexcusable that another driver pulls out in front of you, or opens a door without looking, or a pedestrian crosses between parked cars. But, remember, a good driver is one who can cope with other people's mistakes and accepts that, while ignorance of the rules is no excuse in law, in practice we all bear a responsibility for the safety of everyone else. Remember, we are all capable of making the most dangerous mistakes in a moment of distraction.*

 What is the sequence for changing lanes?

A. Mirrors — signal — manoeuvre. First check all the mirrors and look over my shoulder, if necessary, then signal, if safe, well before moving over.   *Rules 51 & 99*

 What are the rules for lane changing when overtaking or changing direction?

A. 1. I must not move unnecessarily from lane to lane. 2. First use my mirrors to make sure it is safe. 3. If safe, I signal before moving over. 4. I must not make vehicles swerve or slow down.   *Rule 89*

Q What if there isn't enough room for you to move into the other lane? 1. Force a gap. 2. Don't move over. 3. Stop and wait for a gap.

A. 2. I can always find another way back to my route, if I am forced to turn in the wrong direction. If overtaking, I must make sure I don't cause vehicles in front or behind to swerve or slow down. By reading the road ahead and choosing my lane in plenty of time, I can always go the way I want to go, without interfering with anyone else.

Rules 89 & 91

 What do Rules 91 and 103 say about 'jumping queues' in a traffic hold up?

A. It is wrong to jump queues, to overtake, get out of a traffic jam or gain advantage over other drivers who are waiting patiently. It is dangerous because other drivers do no expect me to cut in front of them and so I would refrain from doing so. I may, however, move to a left lane to park or turn left, if another driver acknowledges my signal and lets me into a suitable gap left for me.

Bus and Cycle Lanes

In some towns, but more often cities, you will come across bus lanes. This in itself doesn't pose a major problem, provided you know how to deal with them. They are there to give buses free passage, because, if they needed to join the normal traffic flow they would invariably run a disjointed and late service. Sometimes they run *against* the flow of traffic. Some bus lanes operate for 24 hours, others have an operational time plate showing the day/time/hours you should not enter the lane. Often, cyclists and taxis share these reserved lanes and so you should be especially careful when turning left or right across the lane.

FACT: *Bus lanes are indicated by signs and a solid white line, like this, which separates the lane from the normal road. The words 'and coach' may be added. Sometimes the surface of the bus lane is a different colour from that of the adjacent road.*

Q   What do these signs mean?

1    2    3

 A.   1. There is a bus lane on the road at the next junction, running right to left. I must cross it to turn left or right. 2. It is a bus lane sign. The lane is on the left and may also be used by cyclists. 3. It is an advance notice of a bus lane starting ahead on the same side of the road as me. Cyclists may also use the lane.

 Q   Some bus lanes operate only during specified times. Outside of these times what vehicles are allowed to use the lane? 1. Pedestrians. 2. Cyclists. 3. All vehicles. 4. Only heavy goods vehicles.

A. 3.   *Rule 97*

 Q   Under what circumstances can you never use a bus lane

A.   When the bus lane is physically separated from the rest of the carriageway by a kerbed island.

Q   What should you not do when you see this sign? And why not?

A. I must not park on or near the bus stop. This is because I may hide the signs or cause danger for other vehicles and pedestrians. *Rule 137*

Q Are you allowed to let your vehicle stand in a bus lane? Explain your answer. 1. Yes. 2. Not under any circumstances. 3. Under certain circumstances.

A. 3. I may enter the bus lane and stop to load or unload goods, but only outside the times when there is a specific period of restriction on loading. *Rule 138*

Q What does this sign mean and what is unusual about its message?

A. Contra-flow bus lane. The arrow on the left is my direction of travel, and is a one way traffic sign. However, there is a special lane on the right of my lane for buses to drive toward me, against the normal flow of traffic.

Q The driver of a stationary bus is signalling an intention to pull out. What should you do?

A. Allow the bus to pull out in front of me if I can do so safely. *Rule 79*

FACT: *It is an offence to drive or park a motor vehicle on a cycle lane marked by a solid white line. If the cycle lane is marked by a broken white line, do not enter if you can avoid it. The signs for these lanes are shown in Chapter 3 — The Cyclist.* *Rule 98*

Q Sometimes, buses are excluded from certain roads. When this is the case, this sign will be displayed. What does it mean?

A. No vehicles over 12 seats except regular scheduled school and works services.

15

Types of Road

Single Track, Country Roads

Q You are the driver of a large, slow-moving vehicle travelling along a narrow, winding road. Several vehicles have caught you up and are trying to overtake, but can't. What should you do? 1. Drive faster. 2. Be prepared to pull in. 3. Stay at the same speed. 4. Slow down. 5. Stop.

A. 2. I should pull in and slow down or stop, as soon as the opportunity presents itself. The faster traffic can then pass me.   *Rule 53*

Q What is the main problem with single track roads?

A. The road is only wide enough for single file traffic.   *Rule 82*

Q What happens if you meet another vehicle? 1. There are special passing places. 2. One of us goes into a hedge. 3. You must reverse back to a main road.

A. 1.   *Rule 82*

Q When would you use such passing places? 1. When you see a vehicle coming toward you. 2. When a faster vehicle wants to overtake. 3. Neither of these.

A. 1 and 2.   *Rule 82*

Q Which of the following are relevant to passing places? 1. Park only in passing places. 2. Give way to downhill traffic. 3. Give way to uphill traffic. 4. Never park in passing places.

Q Describe what should happen next by the following statements. Indicate those which are correct.

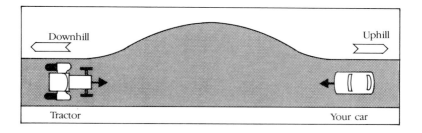

1. You should give way to the tractor. 2. The tractor should give way to you. 3. The farmer should give way because the passing place is on his side. 4. You should wait opposite the passing place. 5. You should cross into the passing place to leave the tractor a straight course. 6. The tractor is travelling downhill. 7. You should allow the tractor free passage wherever possible. 8. You must make the tractor stop.

A. 1, 4 and 7 are correct. The tractor is travelling uphill and I must wait opposite the passing place in any case. Passing places rarely allow room for one vehicle to have complete free passage. The other should therefore pass slowly even when I stop. *Rule 82*

One Way Streets

Q What signs would you be likely to see indicating that the next street is a one way street?

A. If I were at the start of the street I would see the blue rectangular sign with a white arrow and the words 'one way'. If I am passing a one way street which comes into my road either from the left or right, I would see first a 'no left turn' or a 'no right turn' sign, and at the side road itself, 'no entry' signs.

FACT: *Two signs indicating a one way street.*

Q In a two lane one way street, which lane should you use to turn left, turn right and continue straight on?

A. Turning left — I would use the left lane. Turning right — I would use the right lane. To continue straight on — I can use whichever lane is most convenient. *Rule 96*

Q What are the rules for selecting your exit lane? 1. Choose the correct lane early. 2. If you find you're in the wrong lane, stop until someone lets you in. 3. Never change lanes suddenly. 4. Signals aren't necessary in a one way street.

A. 1 and 3. *Rule 96*

Q You are driving along a three lane one way street and want to turn right. Which lane do you use and when do you select it? 1. The left lane. 2. The middle lane. 3. The right lane. (a) Drive along the left and gradually change lanes before the exit. (b) Stay in the right lane. (c) Drive along the centre lane and then change lanes.

A. 3 and (b). However, road markings may indicate that I can use the centre lane for turning right if the right lane is for parking or an early turn off into property. In busy city areas, I must be careful that the right lane isn't a contra-flow bus lane and look for the appropriate signs and solid white line.

Q When driving along a one way street, you notice that traffic on your right is moving more slowly than you. What do you do? 1. Slow down to the same speed. 2. Continue to pass slowly if safe to do so. 3. Sound your horn and pray nobody darts across in front of you.

You turn into a road and notice three lanes of traffic driving towards you. The drivers start flashing their lights at you and you realise, with horror, that you have turned into a one way street. What do you do? 1. Pull over to the side of the road and stop. 2. An emergency stop. 3. A hasty U turn. 4. Keep going slowly until you find a suitable exit.

A. 1 is correct. It is important that I don't panic and, instead, wait until the traffic has cleared, then turn around or reverse into a suitable opening.

Three Lane Undivided Single Carriageway

 What is a three lane single carriageway? 1. A motorway. 2. An ordinary road. 3. A road with a very long lay-by.

A. 2.

 What is the centre lane used for? 1. Overtaking and turning right. 2. Overtaking and turning left. 3. Only for turning right.

A. 1.   *Rule 92*

 Who has priority to use the centre lane, you or oncoming traffic?

A. Neither of us has priority. Either of us may use the lane when it is unoccupied by other traffic.   *Rule 92*

 Can you explain in more detail who can use the centre lane and what the dangers are?

A. Anyone can use the centre lane, when it is safe to do so, for overtaking or turning right. However, the danger occurs if I am not observant enough. Before moving out I must not only look behind and ahead, but also at traffic coming toward me. Has anybody got an indicator on to tell me they are about to overtake and place themselves on collision course with me? Is that car way ahead of me in the middle lane moving, or is the driver waiting to turn right?

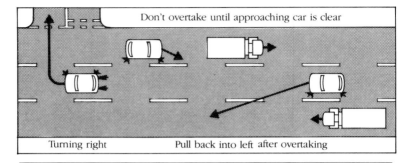

Don't overtake until approaching car is clear

Turning right   Pull back into left after overtaking

Q   On a three lane undivided single carriageway, are you allowed to use the right lane for overtaking? 1. yes, if the road is clear. 2. Only if there is slow traffic in the left and middle lanes. 3. No, never. 4. Yes, if the car in the middle lane wants to turn right.

A. 3. 1, 2 and 4 are not only illegal but dangerous. *Rule 92*

Four or More Lane, Undivided, Single Carriageways

FACT: *On this type of road, the available lanes at any one time will depend on how busy the road is, so that priority is given to the main traffic flows. Signs like this one indicate which lanes are available to traffic facing the sign.*

Here, only two lanes are available (downward pointing arrows), whereas there are three lanes available to traffic from the opposite direction.

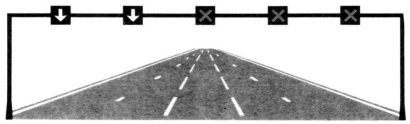

If traffic flows change and your side becomes busier, the centre lane may change from a red cross to a white arrow and the previous sign facing oncoming traffic will change beforehand to look like this one.   *Rule 79*

Q What are the rules for a four lane single carriageway? 1. Use all the lanes at will when overtaking. 2. Do not use the right hand half of the road unless signs and markings indicate that you may do so. 3. Keep in the left lane except when overtaking.

A. 2 and 3.   *Rule 93*

Dual-Carriageways

Q What is the main significance of a dual-carriageway?

A. Opposing streams of traffic are separated by a strip of turf and all the traffic on one side travels in the same direction.

Q On a two lane dual-carriageway how are the lanes used?

A. The left lane is the normal driving lane for traffic and the outside lane is for overtaking or turning right.
                                                               Rule 94

Q Where should you wait to turn right on a dual-carriageway? 1. In the right lane. 2. In the gap in the central reservation. 3. In the left lane. 4. In the acceleration lane.

A. 2. I must also remember to keep clear of traffic on both carriageways and not let my vehicle jut out.   *Rule 112*

Q How can you help a vehicle wishing to merge with the dual-carriageway from the left? 1. Flash your lights. 2. Sound your horn. 3. Move over into the right lane, if you can do so safely.

A. 3.

Q On a three lane dual-carriageway, how should you use each lane? Suggestions: (a) Drive in the left lane for turning left. (b) The middle lane for driving straight on. (c) The outside lane to drive at 70mph.

A. None of the suggested answers is correct.

Inside lane — normal driving lane. Should also be in this lane to turn left.

Middle lane — to overtake slower vehicles. Return to the left lane afterwards.

Outside lane — for overtaking only or for turning right onto right hand deceleration lane. Move back to middle and to left lane after overtaking.   *Rule 95*

 When crossing a dual-carriageway from one side road to another or from a side road and turning right onto the carriageway, how should you treat the move?

A. As two separate movements. First account for traffic from the right and, when safe, move to the central reservation. Then account for traffic from the left before completing the manoeuvre.   *Rule 112*

 What do you do if the central reservation is too small to accept your vehicle safely when you wish to turn right?

A. I must wait in the side road until I can cross into the furthest carriageway in one movement.   *Rule 112*

 What will help you decide whether to turn right in one movement or two? 1. The width of the central reservation. 2. The speed of traffic. 3. The length of my vehicle.

A. 1 and 3. If I am towing a large trailer or driving a lorry, obviously I need a wider sanctuary area in the middle.
                                        Rule 112

Signs at the start and end of a dual-carriageway

NOTE: *Signs. 1. Dual-carriageway ends. 2. 30mph speed limit (may be 40mph). 3. Two-way traffic straight ahead. 4. Keep left. 5. Dual-carriageway or dual-carriageway ahead. 6. National speed limit applies (70mph).*

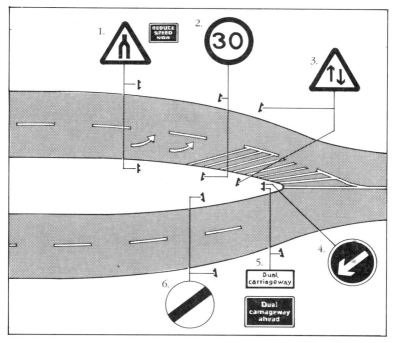

Q Why is it important to take extra notice of the end of a dual-carriageway sign and the two way traffic sign?

A. I am probably travelling fast and need to slow down as I am no longer allowed to travel at 70mph. Indeed the speed restriction may be much lower if I am entering a built up area. If I am overtaking I will need to pull back into the left shortly. I am also entering a road in which traffic will pass on my right. I must be careful that I don't drive too fast while thinking I am fine and inside the speed limit. I must always be wary of the driver behind whose 'speed feeling' hasn't worn off yet and who may try to overtake me.

16
Signs for Routes and Directions

Thanks to the Department of Transport, the system of direction signs in this country is very comprehensive and up to date. It is a simple matter to find your way around the road system, even over extended distances.

 Q Do you know the general pattern and colours of direction signs?
1. Direction signs are mostly _____.
2. Signs on primary routes have _____ backgrounds.
3. Signs on motorways have _____ backgrounds.
4. Signs pointing to motorways from primary routes have _____ backgrounds.
5. Signs on non-primary routes have _____ backgrounds and _____ borders.
6. Local direction signs have _____ backgrounds and _____ borders.
7. Signs for Ministry of Defence establishments have _____ backgrounds and _____ borders.
8. Route signs for pedestrians have _____ backgrounds, white lettering and a symbol.
9. Signs for lorry routes have _____ backgrounds and _____ symbols and lettering.
10. The background of temporary direction signs may be coloured _____, _____ or _____.
11. Traffic diversion signs have _____ backgrounds and _____ lettering.
12. Signs to ancient monuments or National Trust properties have _____ backgrounds with _____ borders and lettering.
13. At the junction, direction signs show your turn by an _____ shape at one end.

A. 1. Rectangular. 2. Green. 3. Blue. 4. Blue. 5. White and black. 6. White and blue. 7. White and red. 8. Blue. 9. Blcak and white. 10. Yellow, blue or white. 11. Yellow and black. 12. Brown and white. 13. Arrow.

Primary Route Signs

Q What is this sign found on primary routes?

A. It is an advance direction sign for a roundabout ahead. The exit straight ahead has a motorway symbol and, therefore, motorway regulations apply from that exit. The motorway shown in brackets (M1) can also be reached by proceeding in that direction.

Q What do you notice about these two primary route signs?

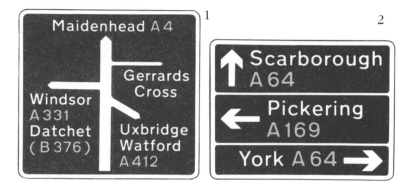

A. 1. Shows the junction layout ahead. The more important the road off the main road, the thicker the line. 2. Found on approach to junctions where space is restricted, when a 'stacking system' of destinations is adopted.

Q Where would these signs be found?

A. 1 is a pointed direction sign which occurs at a junction and marks the turn. 2. is found on faster roads and is sited at the beginning of a deceleration lane, where to use a sign such as 1 would have caused me to miss my turning.

Q What is this sign?

A. It is a route confirmation sign and enables me to confirm that I am still on the correct route for my destination.

NOTE: *Brackets mean — the route number in brackets can be reached by the route preceding it on the sign.*

Q What is this sign?

A. It is a primary traffic route ring road and means that I can avoid congestion in the next town by taking this road.

Q Where would you be likely to see countdown markers like this and what do they represent?

A. Normally I'd expect to see them on fast primary routes where advance warning of a deceleration lane or a roundabout is necessary. They represent distance in hundreds of yards.

Non-Primary Routes

Q Can you explain these non-primary route signs?

 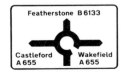 

A. 1 is found on approach to a junction and shows that the B6049, off to the right, has a height restriction of 14ft 6ins.

However, I can still reach Bradwell, with a high vehicle, by forking left, as the brackets indicate another turn off somewhere along the Matlock road. 2. Also an advance direction sign, featuring a roundabout ahead. 3. the minor road, that I am on, crosses a primary traffic route ahead, indicated by the green A38 panels. The more important road also has a thicker line.

 How do these signs differ in their meaning?

A. 1 is a pointed direction sign, sited at a junction to mark the turn. 2 is a non-primary route confirmation sign.

 What do these two signs mean? Pick one meaning for each sign. 1. Roundabout ahead. 2. Reversing lane. 3. Ring road. 4. A happy route. 5. Higher ring road. 6. Holiday route.

A. 1 is found on non-primary ring roads — 3. 2 is a holiday route — 6, these signs being placed on roads which lead to the main holiday destination.

Local Direction Signs

 What can you say about the junction ahead and the sign?

A. The sign is a local direction sign. The stacking system suggests lack of space and is probably in a town area. The junction has four roads leading from it, including my own, with the nearest towns shown in miles.

Q Can you make short notes about each of the following signs?

A. 1. Direction sign showing the turn to a local destination. 2. Direction to toilets for drivers which have disabled facilities. 3. Turn off sign to a railway station for drivers. 4. Direction to caravan and camping site, showing the turn. 5. Direction to public telephones for drivers, showing the turn. 6. Turn off sign to a picnic site for drivers. 7. Direction sign for a car ferry. 8. Turn off sign for Ministry of Defence establishments.

Signs for Pedestrians

Q Where would you see signs like this and what are they?

A. I would be most likely to see these signs in towns, where they show the best route for pedestrians. Drivers may not be able to use such a direct route unless they park somewhere, and walk.

Signs for Lorries

Q Why are there special signs for lorries and why should you, as a driver, be careful about following the same route?

A. Lorry drivers use these symbols because they show the best route for large vehicles to find primary traffic routes, docks or industrial estates. I need to be careful as there may be a higher proportion of lorries on these routes than I would normally meet on the road.

Temporary Traffic Signs

Q Who uses these temporary traffic signs and what makes number three different?

1   2   3

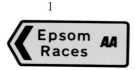  

A. Usually the motoring organisations use these signs to indicate the best route to short term events likely to attract large crowds and much traffic. 3 is a diversion route sign and will be taken away when the normal route is available again.

Signs for Tourists and Places of Interest

Q Can you write below each sign its likely meaning?

1 2   3

4 5 6

A. 1. Tourist information point. 2. Picnic site. 3. Ancient monument. 4. National Trust. 5. Country park. 6. Leisure or sports centre.

NOTE: *These blue tourist signs are gradually being changed to white on brown to make them more distinctive. The pictures will be similar, though.*

Q What are these signs?

1

2

A. 1. Turn off point to an ancient monument. 2. Turn off point to a tourist attraction.

NOTE: *Direction signs like these will be found at junctions and will point to the attraction.*

Thereafter, smaller signs with just a symbol on them will direct the way to the attraction.

Q In addition, new symbols have been designed for tourist destinations. Can you match them up with their probable meaning?

1   2   3

A. Museum.
B. English Heritage.
C. Garden

A. 1 — B. 2 — A. 3 — C.

17

Roundabouts

Q What is the difference between these signs?

1  2

A. 1 is a mini-roundabout sign, placed before the Give Way line. 2 is for larger roundabouts and means roundabout ahead.

Q What is the driver's give-way rule when approaching a roundabout? 1. Give way to traffic approaching from the left. 2. Traffic from the right gives way to you. 3. Give way to all traffic on the right.

A. 3. *Rule 123*

Q Rules for mini-roundabouts are: 1. Slightly different than normal roundbouts? 2. The same as for a crossroads? 3. The same as for larger roundabouts?

A. 3. *Rule 128*

Q What special provision does the Highway Code include about giving priority to traffic on the right and using recommended paths on roundabouts?

A. Give way to traffic on the right unless road markings indicate otherwise. *Rule 123*

NOTE: *The circumstances under which the give way rules may change is shown in the large diagram, shown shortly. The Highway Code gives guidelines for routes to take through roundabouts. These are subject to the approach and exit lanes*

being clear. If blocked, I may use any clearest convenient lane on aproach and exit (shown by a dotted line on diagrams).
Highway Code

 Q Who needs to be shown extra consideration at roundabouts and why?

A. Cyclists and motor cyclists who are more difficult to see anyway, may be moving slower than myself and may select a road position on my left, just before I leave the roundabout. Some lorries, because of their length, may need to enter and use the roundabout in a way that puts me in danger if I am too close, so I should hang back at a distance which will allow the lorry or bus free passage.
Rules 127 & 128

Q Which way does the traffic flow in front of you when facing the roundabout? 1. From left to right. 2. From right to left. 3. Clockwise. 4. Anti-clockwise.

A. 2 and 3.

Q What is the purpose behind roundabouts? Compare them to traffic lights. 1. To keep traffic moving. 2. To save the cost of traffic lights. 3. To make traffic stop?

A. 1. Roundabouts are designed to help me, because traffic in at least one of the entrance roads can always move. This keeps traffic moving and reduces the chances of a major traffic jam.

Junctions controlled by lights have a green light time slot for each road. Even if there's no traffic on it, this can hold up traffic in other roads unnecessarily.

Q The Give Way lines for roads entering a roundabout are: 1. Solid white lines? 2. Single broken lines? 3. Double broken lines? 4. The same as a normal T-junction?

A. 2.

 Q What is a mini-roundabout, what does it look like and how do you use it?

A. It is a very small roundabout and usually quite unlike a normal roundabout. Sometimes the central area may be a small white bump in the road or just a circle of white paint. On approach, I must be prepared to stop and give way at the broken line to traffic on my immediate right. Often these roundabouts are situated where a side road, left as a T-junction, would be congested with traffic. The sign indicates that traffic circulates in a clockwise direction.

FACT: *The road markings for a mini-roundabout look like this. At some locations, the Give Way sign is also shown above the mini-roundabout sign. Then the entrance to the roundabout, on that road, is marked by a double broken line.*

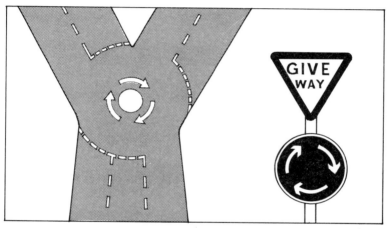

Q What should you do if the roundabout is clear? 1. Stop to make sure. 2. Keep moving. 3. Indicate right.

A. 2.   *Rule 123*

Q What will help you decide whether it is safe to enter the roundabout?

A. By looking at the roundabout early enough, I can assess the traffic on it and decide what is likely to happen before I get there. If traffic is approaching from the right, I must allow it to cross in front of me. I should slow down and select an appropriate gear, ready to pull away again when the traffic clears. If the roundabout is clear, I am already in the correct gear to proceed safely.

Q What is different about the Mirror — Signal — Manoeuvre — Position — Speed — Look routine you would use on approach to a roundabout? 1. Nothing. 2. You use a different routine altogether. 3. Position — Speed — Look comes first.

A. 1. I should use the same sequence to negotiate a roundabout as I would a normal junction. First, I check my mirrors, signal, if safe, and position the car in the correct lane. Next check my speed and slow down if necessary, selecting an appropriate gear for the approach and forward movement. Then I do my observation (look) before completing the manoeuvre.

Q When approaching a roundabout and intending to take the first exit left, you should: 1. Signal left on approach? 2. Not give a signal? 3. use the right lane? 4. Use the left lane? 5. keep to the left lane on roundabout? 6. Signal after you pass the first exit? 7. Leave in the left lane when possible?

A. 1, 4, 5 and 7. *Rule 124*

Q When approaching a roundabout and intending to take the road straight ahead, you should: 1. Signal left on approach? 2. Not give a signal? 3. Only go straight on if there is a middle lane? 4. Use the left lane normally? 5. Cross to right lane in roundabout? 6. Use right lane if necessary? 7. Signal left when passing last exit before leaving? 8. Signal right to leave roundabout?

A. 2, 4,6 and 7. *Rule 124*

Q When approaching a roundabout and intending to turn right, you should: 1. Not signal on approach? 2. Signal left on approach? 3. Use the left lane all the way round? 4. Change to right lane on roundabout? 5. Signal right? 6. Approach in the right lane? 7. Move across to right (inside) lane? 8. Always leave in right lane? 9. Keep to inside lane on roundabout? 10. Change to left signal after last exit before leaving?

Signals to give and paths to use at roundabouts

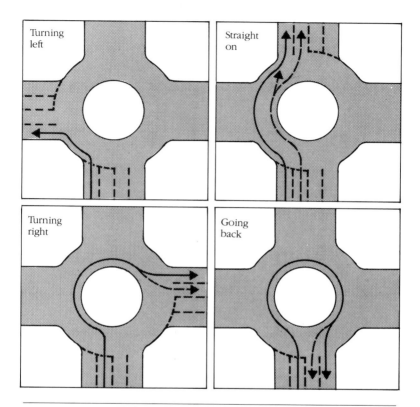

Q Who should receive your special consideration on roundabouts?

A. Vehicles which are crossing in front of me and leaving by the next exit. Also cyclists, motor cyclists and large lorries. *Rule 125*

Q It is recommended that you leave a roundabout in the left hand lane. When is it proper to leave in the right-hand lane? 1. Anytime. 2. When the left lane is blocked. 3. To overtake.

A. 2. *Highway Code*

Roundabout Summary for a Two Lane Entrance

	Turning left	*Going straight on*	*Turning right*
Approach signal	Left indicator	No signal	Right indicator
Approach lane	Left lane	Left lane	Right lane
Roundabout lane	Outside lane	Outside lane	Inside lane
Change signal	No change	Signal left on passing last exit	Maintain right signal until passing exit before leaving, change to left signal
Exit lane	Left lane unless blocked	Left lane unless blocked	Left lane unless blocked

Rules 124

Q Where there are more than two lanes at the entrance to a roundabout, which lane do you select?

A. First, I must see, by looking at the route signs, which exit I should take and then use the clearest convenient lane suitable for that exit, both on approach and throughout the roundabout. For example, if I want to turn left, I use the left lane. The middle lane is for going straight on. For turning right, I'd use the right lane. This assumes that signs and road markings don't indicate otherwise. *Rule 124*

Where there is more than one roundabout, the same rules apply, but keep a lookout in case there are Give Way lines.

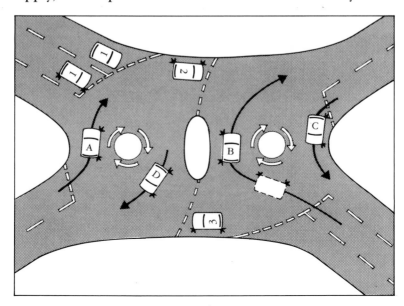

The two number 1 cars are both giving way to A who is going over to the second roundabout. Number 2 is giving way to B. Notice the change of signal. C has started to pull out, the reason being, number 2 has stopped for car B. Number 2 also has a left signal on which suggests the driver will take the first exit. C's move is the result of B still being on the other side of the roundabout and not because of B's signal. Number 3 is giving way to D, who is leaving at the next exit.

Occasionally, although a merger of several roads appears to be a roundabout, one or major roads may be allowed clear passage throughout, and it is the vehicles *on the roundabout* which must give way. When this occurs, there will be Give Way signs and the road will be marked with double broken lines, just like a normal junction.

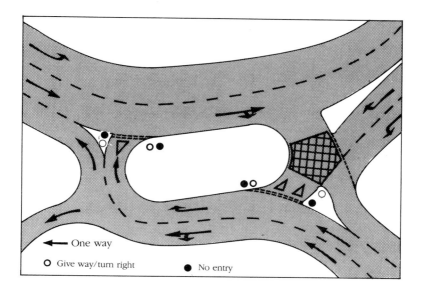

← One way

O Give way/turn right   ● No entry

18

Box Junctions

Q What do criss-cross yellow lines at a junction, with a yellow line border, indicate? 1. No parking at the junction. 2. No entry. 3. You can ignore traffic light signals if your exit is clear. 4. A box junction.

A. 4.

Q What are the rules for entering a box junction, when you want to go straight on and for turning left?

A. I must not enter the area of the box if the lane that I will use to exit from it is blocked by other traffic.   *Rule 113*

Q At a box junction, you may wait in the box if: 1. The lane you want to leave by has traffic in it? 2. The traffic lights are green? 3. You want to turn right? 4. You want to turn left? 5. Traffic is queueing across the box?

A. 3.   *Rule 113*

FACT: *You should never enter a box junction area unless it is safe for you to do so. Once you are in, keep looking and get across as quickly as you can without racing.*

Q You are approaching a box junction in the right hand lane and want to turn right. The vehicle in front of you is also indicating to turn right. The lights change to green, for you and the vehicles on the opposite side. The car in front moves forward into the box and stops. You follow and wait behind. Okay?

A. That depends. If there are only a couple of cars at the opposite set of lights and they don't want to cross my path, I could very slowly approach the car in front because it will likely be there for only a few seconds. If the traffic blocking my path is heavy, I would certainly wait at my lights and allow a sufficient gap between me and the car in front, so that I don't block the path of other vehicles also turning right from the opposite side.

Q You want to turn right, your way forward to a right turn position is clear, but your entrance to the side road is blocked by cars, backed up to the junction. Are you correct in pulling forward and waiting for the side road to be clear? 1. Yes. 2. No. 3. If your lights are green. 4. If you have priority.

A. 2. No. If the exit doesn't clear before the lights change again, I would be putting myself and my passengers at risk from collision. I would be blocking the junction and forcing traffic to negotiate their way around me.

 Look at the diagram, and using the previous answers as a guide, judge whether the numbered cars are correct in their use of the box junction?

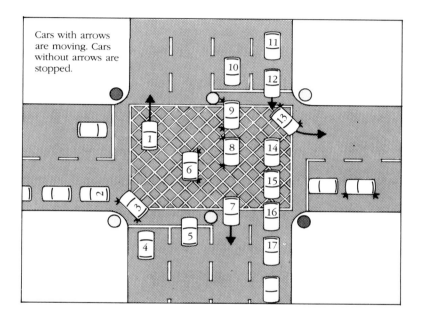

Cars with arrows are moving. Cars without arrows are stopped.

A. 1. Yes, the exit is clear. 2. yes, the car is off the box. 3. No, car blocking junction and exit not clear. 4. Yes, holding back. 5. Yes, if car goes no further. 6. Yes, positioned correctly. 7. Yes, the exit is clear. 8. No, exit is blocked, car now blocking junction. 9. No, should not follow 8, exit is blocked and blocking path of 6. 10, Yes, should wait here. 11. Yes, should wait here. 12. No, cars in front are stationary. 13. Yes, exit is clear, can just pass behind 14. 14. No, exit not clear, now blocking junction. 15. No, exit not clear, now blocking junction. 16. No, exit not clear, half on half off, but better than 15. 17. Yes, managed to clear box junction.

19

Railway Level Crossings

 What is a level crossing and what would you find at one?

A. A level crossing is a point at which railway lines and a road cross each other at the same place. Generally, I will see warning signs on approach and a full or half barrier which will close when a train is due to pass.

Q There are four types of level crossing and the designs usually reflect the amount of traffic which uses the road. Do you know what the differences are?

A. There are: 1. Level crossings with gates or full barriers. 2. Automatic half-barrier level crossings. 3. Automatic open crossings, and 4. Open level crossings.

FACT: *All types of crossing are designed to interrupt the flow of road traffic as little as possible. Negotiated properly, traffic can cross safely, but during the times when a train needs to use the crossing, your continued safety relies on your knowing the rules and acting properly on signals and signs which show on approach.*

General Rules for all Types of Level Crossing

 What is the most important rule to remember when negotiating a level crossing? 1. Always give way to trains. 2. Only stop if the lights are red. 3. Always phone the signalman first.

A. 1.

 What are the important rules to apply when driving over a level crossing? Think of speed, gaps and visibility.

A. 1. I must approach at a moderate speed. 2. Look in order to check that the lines are actually clear before crossing. 3. Never loiter on the crossing. 4. Drive over

quickly, but without racing. 5. Never drive 'nose to tail' over the crossing. 6. Never proceed unless I can see the road on the other side is clear for me. 7. Never stop on the crossing between the barriers or gates. 8. Move away from the exit after crossing so that I don't force anyone to stop behind me. 9. If the crossing contains box junction markings, I must not enter until my exit is clear. (Rule 113, first half.)
Rule 225

 What three incidents may occur on a level crossing which have the potential to be very dangerous?

A. I may stall, break down or be involved in an accident with another vehicle, which causes me to remain in the crossing area for longer than is safe. *Rule 230*

 If your vehicle breaks down on a level crossing, there are very clear guidelines for the events which should follow. Can you place them in the correct order? 1. Try to move the vehicle if the lights and alarms haven't started. 2. If the alarms sound, or the lights show, stand well clear of the crossing. 3. Get all passengers out of the vehicle and clear of the crossing. 4. Telephone the signalman again if you manage to get off the crossing. 5. Telephone the signalman immediately using the phone provided.

A. (a) — 3. (b) — 5. (c) — 1. (d) — 4. (e) — 2.
Rule 230
Now read them through in the correct order, so the sequence is clear.

 In addition to lights, what other signal will you get which also means stop? 1. An audible alarm. 2. Flashing amber lights. 3. The barrier will drop.

A. 1. The audible alarm sounds when the amber light is showing. *Rule 226*

 Most modern level crossings have steady amber and twin flashing red traffic lights, as overleaf. The steady amber light comes on first. What does it mean? 1. Get ready to stop. 2. You have one minute to cross. 3. Stop unless unsafe.

This is followed by the flashing red lights, what do them mean? 1. You only have 15 seconds to cross. 2. Stop at the line. 3. Stop crossing as the barriers drop.

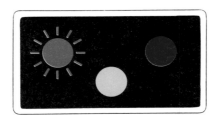

A. Steady amber means I must stop at the white line if safe to do so, number 3. Flashing red means I must stop at the white line as a train is coming and the barriers will soon be lowered, number 2. *Rule 226*

Q What are the correct meanings of these signs?

a   b   c   d   e

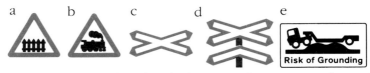

1. Long low trailered vehicles may become stuck. 2. Only steam engines use this line. 3. Level crossing without barrier or gate ahead. 4. (St Andrew's cross) Level crossing without barrier. 5. Road ahead blocked with gates. 6. (St Linda's cross) With full barrier. 7. Level crossing without barrier but with more than one railway line. 8. Level crossing with barrier or gate ahead.

A. (a) — 8. (b) — 3. (c) — 4. (d) — 7. (e) — 1.

Automatic Half-Barrier Level Crossings

Q At an automatic half-barrier level crossing the barriers fall across which side of the road? 1. The left side. 2. The right side. 3. Across all of the road.

A. 1.   *Rules 226 & 228*

Q Who or what operates an automatic half-barrier level crossing? 1. The leading car approaching the crossing. 2. The approaching train. 3. The signalman overseeing the crossing.

A. 2.

 Q Shortly before reaching the crossing, a train triggers the events which warn that it is coming. What happens?

A. First I will see steady amber warning lights and hear an audible alarm. Then the red Stop lights will begin to flash when the barriers are about to come down. *Rule 226*

 Q What must you do if on approach to a level crossing the amber light comes on and a bell is ringing? 1. Stop. 2. Keep going until the lights change to red. 3. Stop unless it is unsafe to do so.

A. 3.

 Q Suppose you have just started to cross and the amber light and bell starts working, what should you do then? 1. Keep going. 2. Stop at the railway lines. 3. Do a U turn.

A. 1. *Rule 226*

 Q If the signals continue after a train has passed, what do you do?

A. Wait. Another train will be passing soon. *Rule 227*

Q Where do you wait when the amber light is on or the red lights flash and the barrier is down? 1. Passengers wait at the side of the road. 2. At the zig-zag lnes. 3. At the white Stop line.

A. 3.

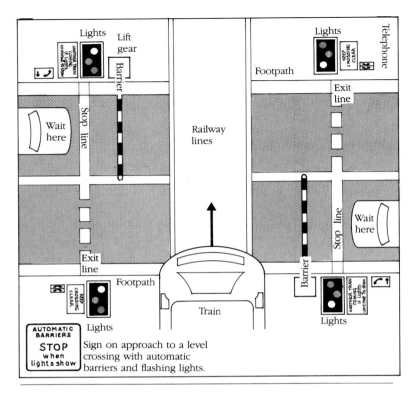

Sign on approach to a level crossing with automatic barriers and flashing lights.

AUTOMATIC BARRIERS
STOP when lights show

Q If you are on foot, where do you wait?

A. I would wait at the footpath near the barrier, or the broken white line alongside the Stop line.

Q The train has gone by, but the barriers remain down and the red lights keep flashing. What has gone wrong? 1. The signalman has fallen asleep. 2. There is another train coming. 3. The system has broken down.

A. 2. Nothing has gone wrong. I must wait for the second train before the barrier will lift.   *Rule 227*

Q What must you never do at an automatic half-barrier level crossing and why not?

A. I must never zig-zag around the barriers under any

circumstances. I could be killed, and would be endangering the lives of my passengers and also British Rail passengers.

Rule 228

Q The main danger when moving over any type of crossing is the speed at which you cross. With this in mind, what should the drivers of large, slow moving vehicles or herdsmen do, before driving vehicles or animals over railway crossings? 1. Telephone the signalman for permission. 2. Ask for police protection. 3. Cross and hope the barriers don't come down.

A. 1.

NOTE: *There is a phone directly connected to the signalman at the crossing for this purpose.* *Rules 229 & 230*

Q What should the driver of a large, slow moving vehicle or a herdsman do once across and clear of the crossing?

A. If the telephone has been used to inform the signalman before crossing, then it is logical to ring again, confirming a safe passage, and that the crossing is now clear.

Rule 229

FACT: *These two signs before a crossing indicate a requirement to telephone for authority to proceed.* Large *means vehicles over 55ft long or 9ft 6ins wide or 38 tonnes total weight.* Slow *means vehicles which cannot cross faster than 5mph.* Low *means vehicles with a low slung trailer, like a transporter, which may become lodged over the tracks.*

Drivers of
LARGE or SLOW
VEHICLES
must phone
and get permission
to cross

LARGE means
over 55′ long or 9′-6″ wide
or 38 tonnes total weight
SLOW means 5mph or less

Risk of Grounding

DRIVERS OF LONG
LOW VEHICLES
phone
before crossing

Q You have been waiting patiently at the barrier for several minutes without seeing any sign of a train, what should you do next? 1. Complain to British Rail. 2. Phone the signalman and ask for advice. 3. Drive around the barriers and look carefully before crossing.

A. 2.

Automatic Open Crossings

Q What is an automatic open crossing and what will you find there?

A. Automatic open crossings have no barriers, gates or an attendant. Control of the road traffic is by the use of amber lights, an audible alarm and flashing red Stop lights.

Rule 234

FACT: *These are the signs that you will see on approach to an automatic open crossing. The St Andrew's cross is used at all crossings which do not have gates or barriers. An additional cross half, below the main cross, means more than one line of railway.*

Q What are the rules governing your use of these crossings?

A. 1. When the lights show and alarm sound I must stop and wait. 2. Do not start to cross as a train will arrive shortly. 3. If the lights continue to flash after the train has gone by, I must wait for another train. 4. If am driving a large slow vehicle (or herding animals), I must phone the signalman first. 5. Once across I must inform the signalman that I am clear by phoning again.

 As there are no barriers which will lift away from the road, how do you know when it is safe to proceed? 1. An alarm will sound. 2. The lights will go out. 3. The green Go light will come on.

A. 2.

NOTE: *There are no green Go lights at these crossings and it should be safe to proceed when the Stop lights go out.*

Rule 227

Level Crossings with Gates or Full Barriers

FACT: *There are several types of gated or full barriered level crossings.*
1. Some have an attendant or are controlled remotely, and go right across the road, with amber lights and an alarm, followed by flashing red Stop lights. Occasionally there are no lights at all.
2. Some will have no attendant and are controlled by miniature red and green traffic lights.
3. Others have no attendant or red lights, but do have a special railway telephone.

 If you encountered a level crossing like number 1, how would you negotiate it?

A. If the crossing has an attendant the gates will be opened and closed for me whenever there are no trains due. If there are lights I must not pass them once they show, just as for the automatic half-barrier crossings. Where there are no lights at all, I must stop when the gates begin to close or the barriers gently descend, as a train will shortly reach the crossing.

 Approaching a level crossing with gates or barriers but no attendant (number 2) you will see these signs. What do you do when the green light is on? 1. Close the gates or lower barriers before driving away from the far side.

2. Open both gates fully or raise both barriers until upright. 3. Switch off your engine and get out of your vehicle. 4. Stop at the gates or barriers. 5. Check that green light is still on before driving across.

A. 4, 3, 2, 5 and 1. Read through the correct sequence again.

NOTE: *Do not attempt to open the gates if the red light is on.*

NOTE: *The telephone rules about larger, slow moving vehicles and herding animals, remain the same.*   *Rule 229*

 Q You are approaching (number 3) an unmanned level crossing which has gates, but no lights. There is, however, a railway telephone. Describe how you would negotiate this type of level crossing.

A. First, I would stop, get out, look both ways and listen for trains. Then, I would use the special railway telephone and contact the signalman to make sure a train wasn't due shortly. Next, I open both gates wide and check again that no train is coming. After driving over and when clear of the crossing, I must close both gates behind me. Lastly, I phone the signalman to say that I am clear.   *Rule 233*

FACT: *At a fully gated level crossing with entrance and exit gates, always open both gates before crossing. NEVER stop halfway over to open the exit gate, as this would be highly dangerous.*   *Rule 232*

Q What are these signs and where would you see them?

A. These signs are countdown markers placed on approach to a concealed level crossing after the first warning sign to the crossing. Each represents one third of the distance from the sign to the crossing, and are approximately 100 yards apart.

Open Level Crossings

 What is an open level crossing?

A. Open level crossings are those with no gates, barriers, attendant or traffic lights at all. Traffic must give way to trains.

 Where you see this red, white and black sign there is an open level crossing ahead. What must you do before crossing?

A. I must stop before looking both ways and listening for trains. By stopping, my engine noise will be quieter at idle and by winding down the window I can listen effectively, before crossing. The rules state I must give way to trains.   *Rule 234*

Horse Riders at Level Crossings

 What rules should horse riders use at level crossings? 1. The same rules as for other vehicles. 2. Their own rules. 3. Dismount and walk across. 4. Gallop across.

A. 1. Riders should note that when the audible warning sounds, they should stop well back from the alarm and track area. Because your horse must be kept under control, do not dismount. If you have started to cross when the warnings sound, keep going and try to be well away from the crossing before the train arrives, there is still plenty of time to get clear at normal pace.

20

Signals by Drivers to Others

Q When would you be correct in giving signals to others? 1. If they would help or warn others. 2. All the time, whichever way you go. 3. If they would confuse a driver. 4. They're only really necessary if you are turning right.

A. 1. Give signals if they would help or warn other road users. *Rule 45*

Q There are two ways that you can give signals. What are they? 1. Arm signals and brake lights. 2. Direction indicators and hazard lights. 3. Arm signals and direction indicators.

A. 3.

Q There are three rules for giving direction indicator signals, what are they?

A. 1. Give only the correct signal. 2. Give it in good time. 3. If it doesn't self cancel, turn it off. *Rule 45*

Q What three points are relevant when giving arm signals?

A. 1. Give only the correct signal. 2. Give it clearly and for long enough. 3. Give it in time so that I can bring my arm back in for the move. *Rule 45*

TIP: *Use the full length of your arm to give hand signals so that following drivers can see you clearly.*

Q You should always watch out for signals from other drivers and road users, but, what should you do about them? 1. Recognise them quickly. 2. Forget them promptly. 3. Take any necessary action promptly. 4. Obey them.

A. 3. *Rule 46*

Q Though you act on drivers' signals promptly, should you rely on them as being correct?

A. No, especially if my response to their signal means crossing in front of the vehicle. I am still responsible for my own safety. Rule 111

Q When you see these indicator signals on a car or a motorcycle, what is the driver trying to make you aware of?

1  2  3

A. 1. I intend to move out to the right or turn right. 2. I intend to move in to the left or turn left or stop on the left. 3. I am slowing down or stopping.

TIP: *Rely only on the signals of a police officer or traffic warden which, of course, must be obeyed.* *Rule 47*

Q Assuming that you don't give an arm signal, what automatic signal do you have which informs drivers behind that you are slowing down or stopping?

A. My brake lights.

Q What do these arm signals mean?

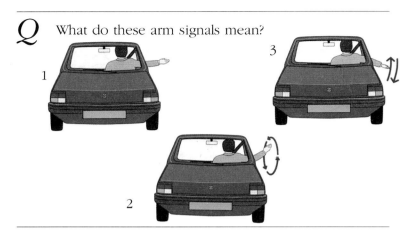

A. 1. I intend to move out to the right or turn right. 2. I intend to move in to the left or turn left. 3. I intend to slow down or stop.

Q Who else should use these arm signals when on the road?

A. Pedal cyclists and those in charge of horses.

Q When is the slowing down arm signal particularly important and why? 1. At traffic lights on red. 2. At a Zebra crossing. 3. In a traffic jam. 4. At roundabouts.

A. 2. Because as well as the vehicle behind, pedestrians need to know that I have seen them and am stopping to give way. I have no forward light indication of braking similar to those at the rear.

Q If the driver in front is giving you a slowing down arm signal, is it safe to overtake? Give a reason for your answer.

A. No. I must check all round before overtaking. Someone may be overtaking me, or the driver may be pulling up at a Zebra crossing, or he may be stopping for some other obstruction (a stray dog perhaps).

21

*T*he Safety of Pedestrians at the Roadside

 Who are most at risk dut to your actions as a driver and what are they depending on?

A. Pedestrians. They depend on me to recognise their vulnerability and ensure their safety.

 How can you show awareness and anticipation for pedestrians? 1. By braking harshly. 2. By driving carefully and slowing down. 3. By increased use of the horn.

A. 2.   *Rule 63*

 At what places, especially, do pedestrians need to be shown extra consideration?

A. When I am approaching crossings or driving along crowded shopping streets where crossings are infrequent. At junctions and roundabouts, because not all pedestrians look all around all of the time, where there is no pavement for them to use, and where the road is unusually narrow for me.   *Rule 63*

 What type of pedestrians need your consideration most, and why?

A. 1. The blind. 2. Those who are both deaf and blind. 3. Young children. 4. The elderly. 5. The disabled or infirm.

Those with hearing difficulties may rely on sight alone to detect my vehicle approaching. The blind place their trust in guide dogs or a white stick and can easily become disorientated at junctions or in noisy traffic. The elderly and the young have particular difficulty in judging the speed and distance of approaching traffic and can take much longer to walk across the road.   *Rule 64*

FACT: *Statistically, two out of every three pedestrians killed or seriously injured on the roads are either under 15 or over 60. Watch out for them.*

Q What do these two signs mean?

1    2

A. 1. Pedestrians on the road ahead. 2. Crossing point for elderly people (the plate may otherwise read blind or disabled).

Q When may pedestrians not be giving traffic their full concentration?

A. When they are shopping, either in a busy high street or at the side of a road at a mobile shop.

Q What sort of door-to-door delivery vehicles should you be wary of when they are stationary and why?

A. Milk floats, mobile fruit and vegetable shops, mobile libraries, ice cream vans, delivery vans, coal lorries and mobile fish and chip vans. Buses can also be included in this list. I am unlikely to want to wait for them so I am going to overtake. I must be careful about people in the vicinity who are more interested in their purchases than my vehicle.   *Rule 63*

Q Where should you be most careful to look because of the danger of pedestrians choosing an unsuitable place to cross?

A. I need to be extra careful around parked or stopped vehicles as a pedestrian may step out unexpectedly.

Rule 63

Q 1. Blind people carry a red/white/green stick. 2. Blind and deaf people carry a yellow/blue/white stick with two red/green/black reflectorised bands. Which colours do not apply?

A. Blind people use white sticks. Blind/deaf people cary white sticks with two red reflective bands.   *Rule 64*

Q On busy streets full of shoppers there are special dangers. What are they and how can you prepare for them?

A. 1. Pedestrians may step off the kerb. 2. Jostling may cause someone to fall into the road. 3. Cycles and cyclists may fall into may path. 4. Car doors can be opened suddenly. I can keep away from the pavement a little further than normal and slow down. By being extra vigilant in my observations I can reduce the chances of an accident.

FACT: *The words 'I never had a chance' are not only useless to the relatives of an accident victim, they are quite often not true. If you drive carefully and keep your eyes open, looking well ahead and behind, always thinking what might happen next and preparing for it, there is every likelihood that you will always have every chance.*

Q You intend to turn left into the next side road and are just at the turn when you spot a pram being shoved into the road in front of you. What do you do? 1. Weave round. 2. Feel sorry for the child. 3. Do an emergency stop. 4. Give way. 5. Tap lightly on the horn.

A. 4. I must give way to pedestrians who are crossing the road into which I am turning, though whoever shoved the pram into the road is not acting correctly.

Rules 11 & 68

Q What special rule applies if the same thing happens when you want to turn right into the next side road?

A. There is no special rule, in fact, Rule 68 applies to turning left or turning right.   *Rule 68*

Q When should you give way to pedestrians who are on the pavement?

A. When I want to enter or emerge from property bordering a road and need to cross over a pavement, such as into a garage forecourt   *Rule 69*

Q Where a pedestrian appears not to have seen you and walks out in front of you, what should you do? 1. Tap lightly on the horn. 2. Give a good blast on the horn. 3. Flash your lights. 4. Rev your engine by slipping the clutch.

A. If I am far enough back, a quick tap ill be enough to alert the pedestrian to my presence. If I am close and there isn't time, my first priority is to stop safely. By striving to anticipate the actions of others I already will be prepared for such an event.

Q Who is most likely to dash across the road in front of you and what must you do for them?

A. Children. I must think for them and help to keep them safe. A running child is a danger signal, as children have a habit of altering course without warning. Again, when I see children, I must prepare myself by slowing down, ready to take safe action.

Q What problems do processions or marching groups pose and how should you deal with them?

A. They often walk in the road and through necessity move quite slowly. If they have a responsible leader, they will be on the left of the road and carrying lights at night. I must give them plenty of room and slow down. I may come upon them suddenly and so should be especially careful on a left hand bend.   *Rule 70*

22

The Safety of Pedestrians at Crossings

Near Schools

Q What should you remember to do when driving past a school?

A. I must drive slowly and carefully near schools and look out for children crossing unsupervised or getting on or off a bus. I must also stop when signalled to do so by a school crossing patrol showing a 'STOP-CHILDREN' sign.

Rules 65 & 66

TIP: *Whenever you pass a school sign, think of the approximate time or look at your clock. School areas are usually busy between 08.30 - 09.15 and between 14.00 - 15.30, though some children may be around at other times also.*

Q Do you always have to stop for a school crossing patrol? 1. Only if you feel generous. 2. Only when the amber lights are flashing. 3. Yes, always. 4. No, never.

A. 3. Yes, I am actually breaking the law if I don't stop when ordered to do so.

The Road User & the Law

Q What other warning may you occasionally find below the school sign?

A. Sometimes in areas of faster traffic or in crowded areas I may see flashing amber lights which are switched on when children are crossing under supervision by a patrol.

Rules 65 & 66

Q This road marking is found outside school entrances and at school crossing patrols. Under what circumstances are you allowed to park there? 1. During school holidays. 2. At any time, but only for two minutes. 3. Only to drop children and pick them up from school. 4. None of these.

A. 4. The rules are that this area should be kept clear at all times and I must not stop or wait — even to pick up or set down children or other passengers.   *Highway Code*

Q What do these signs mean?

1    2    3

A. 1. School crossing patrol; vehicles must stop at the sign. 2. Children going to and from school. 3. School crossing patrol ahead.

Q What does this sign mean, where will you find it and what information plate will there be underneath?

A. Road humps ahead. They are often found around school areas, and other places, to keep the speed of the traffic down. Below the sign there is a plate indicating the distance over which the humps extend.

Zebra Crossings

FACT: *Here is an overhead view of the road marking used at a Zebra crossing.*

 What is the main rule for a Zebra crossing?

A. Zebra crossings may be regarded as extensions of the footpath across the road and therefore pedestrians have right of way when on a crossing.

 When approaching a Zebra crossing, what should you be looking for and thinking about?

A. I should be looking for pedestrians waiting to cross and approach with caution. Children, the elderly, the disabled and the infirm and mothers with prams need my particular consideration. I must always be ready to slow down and stop, and remember that I will need more room for this on wet or icy roads. If there is another vehicle behind, the driver will need an arm signal. *Rule 71*

 What does this sign mean?

A. Pedestrian crossing ahead.

Q On approach to a Zebra crossing there is a signal you can give when you intend to give way. What is it? 1. A left turn signal. 2. An arm signal. 3. A right turn signal. 4. A brake light signal.

A. 2.

 Q What arm signal? What are you trying to say and to whom?

A. I should give a clear slowing down arm signal. I am telling drivers behind that I am slowing down and/or stopping, so that they don't just have my brake lights to rely on. Also pedestrians will see me and be assured that I have seen them waiting at the crossing.

 Q What other signal should you give a pedestrian when giving way for them at a Zebra crossing? 1. Beckon them across the road. 2. Wave to them. 3. Flash your lights. 4. Sound your horn.

A. None of these is correct. I must never signal to a pedestrian. I may be perfectly willing to stop for them, but another vehicle may not, or the driver may not have seen them. I may be beckoning them into danger.   *Rule 71*

Q Must you give way when a pedestrian is waiting on the pavement at a crossing? 1. No. 2. Yes, every time. 3. Only if they are on a cycle.

A. A pedestrian claims priority by placing a foot on the crossing. Immediately this occurs, the pedestrian has right of way. However, I should still anticipate that they are going to cross and be ready to stop if necessary.

Rules 11 & 71

TIP: *Normally this seems fine because it reduces the need for vehicles to stop unnecessarily, when pedestirans are waiting near a crossing, but don't actually want to cross. However, think of the elderly who may be too nervous to do this or the mother who is pushing a pram and can't step forward far enough. Help them by stopping anyway.*

Q What are the zig-zag lines for on both sides of a Zebra crossing? There are several answers, all to do with the safety of pedestrians.

A. 1. I must not park anywhere on the crossing or the zig-zag lines. 2. I must not overtake the moving vehcile nearest the crossing. 3. I must not overtake the leading vehicle stopped at a crossing which is giving way to pedestrians.
Rules 72, 138 and The Road User & the Law

Q What if there are no zig-zag lines? 1. You may overtake. 2. You may park. 3. You must not overtake.

A. 3. I must never overtake just before a crossing.
Rule 72

Q The Give Way lines at a Zebra crossing are: 1. A single broken white line? 2. A double broken white line? 3. A solid white line. They are about: (a) One foot, (b) One metre (c) Three metres from the crossing?

A. 1 and (b).

Q Are you allowed to stop in the zig-zag area of a Zebra crossing?

A. Yes, of course, if I am giving way to a pedestrian. Otherwise I may stop there to avoid an accident when necessary.

Q You are in a queue of traffic which is moving by repeated stops and starts. You come upon a Zebra crossing and stop on the crossing for about 30 seconds before being able to move on again. What have you done wrong?

A. I must always leave the actual crossing area clear and not drive onto it unless I can clear it. This requires me to wait only until the car in front has moved on from the crossing a few yards.
Rule 73

Q How do you deal with a Zebra crossing which has an island in the middle? 1. As one crossing. 2. As two crossings. 3. As a roundabout.

A. 2. I treat it the same way as the pedestrians, as two separate crossings. One on each side of the island.

Rule 13

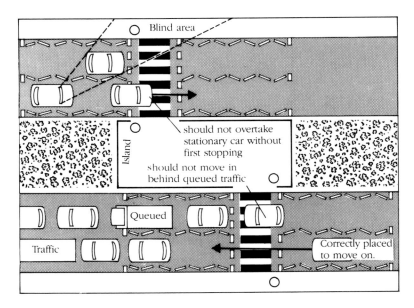

Pelican Crossings

 Q How many types of pedestrian crossing are there and what are they?

A. There are two types — Zebra crossings and Pelican crossings.

Q What is a Pelican crossing?

A. It is a type of crossing controlled by lights, which are operated by the pedestrian.

Q How else may crossings be controlled, besides by lights?
1. By alarms. 2. By a police officer. 3. By a traffic warden.

A. 2 and 3.

Q What should you do when you receive the signal to move on? 1. Just go. 2. Give way to pedestrians still on the crossing. 3. Creep forward slowly to make pedestrians hurry up.

A. 2. *Rule 75*

Q What is the sequence of lights at a Pelican crossing?

A. Green, amber, red, flashing amber, green.

Q When you see the flashing amber signal, what does it mean? 1. Stop. 2. Proceed. 3. Give way to pedestrians on the crossing. 4. Give way to pedestrians on the pavement. 5. Proceed if the crossing is clear.

A. 3 and 5 are correct. *Rule 74*

Q When a straight Pelican crossing has a central refuge, do you treat it like a Zebra crossing with an island? 1. No. 2. Yes. 3. Only if the lights don't work.

A. 1. A straight Pelican crossing is one crossing even if there is a central refuge. I must wait for people crossing from the far side. The only time Pelicans are treated separately is when the crossings are staggered and have separate lights for each side of the island. *Rule 74*

FACT: *Pelican crossings have a double line of metal studs marking the approach. It is an offence to wait or park between these studs and the far side of the crossing area.*

Q What does the Highway Code say about harassing pedestrians at crossings?

A. It is a very dangerous practice because I can startle them and cause them to rush into the path of another moving vehicle. This includes unwarranted use of the horn and revving my engine. *Rule 74*

23
*E*mergency Vehicles

Never unnecessarily inhibit the progress of an emergency vehicle. You never know, next time it may be coming to your aid.

Q Name three types of emergency vehicle you may encounter on the road.

A. Fire engines, ambulances and the police. *Rule 76*

Q How would you know they were approaching during an emergency and what should you do about it?

A. I would hear a two-tone horn, siren or bells sounding and see their flashing blue lights. I must make way for them during an emergency.

Rule 25

Q What should you do about an emergency vehicle which you seen in your mirror or approaching from the front?

A. First, I look at the road ahead and allow the vehicle to pass at the first safe opportunity, without stopping suddenly. If it is approaching from ahead I can give it clear passage by keeping well over on my own side of the road.

Q There is another vehicle which can carry a flashing green lamp during emergencies. Do you know what it is?

A. A doctor's vehicle, when answering an emergency call.

Q What should pedestrians do if you hear or see emergency vehicles?

A. Keep out of the road. *Rules 25 & 76*

SUMMARY: *Where the road is wide it is relatively easy to give way to emergency vehicles by pulling over. Where the road is narrow, don't slow down or stop, but keep going until you find a suitable turn off or passing place. How many times have you seen a car pull over on the brow of a hill, near a narrow bridge or near road islands? The fire chief of a local station told me 'regularly' when I rang to ask him. 'It's natural that drivers want to slow down and let us pass, but choosing an unsuitable place can actually hold us up even more. It's quite exasperating when lives are at stake', he said. So think before you give way.*

Q What does this sign (white letters on a blue ground) mean?

A. Hospital ahead.

Q Where would you find a fire hydrant?

A. Near the side of a road, on the pavement, in some built up areas and outside factories. The fire brigade need to tap into these in the event of a large fire in shopping areas, where many lives may be at risk and larger quantities of water are required. It is important that I do not park near one so that it is readily available at all times.

24

Speed Limits

Q What are the meanings of these signs?

1 2 3 4

A. 1. Minimum speed limit 30mph. 2. Maximum speed limit 40mph. 3. End of minimum speed limit. 4. National speed limit applies.

FACT: *In addition, you may come across signs for 20mph when the roads have been gritted and there are loose chippings flying up from tyres, or occasionaly, 50mph on main roads where a few houses are scattered along the roadside.*

Q If you are a learner driver, by how much do you reduce all of the speed limits that apply to experienced drivers? 1. By 10%. 2. By a quarter. 3. By nothing. 4. By 15%.

A. 3. Learner drivers may drive at the same speeds which apply to everyone else.

Q What rule must you remember about speed limits?

A. First I must obey the speed limits which are indicated by signs along the road and also any overall top speed which applies to the vehicle I am driving (see the owner's manual). *Rules 54 & 55*

Q What extremely important consideration should you remember when driving at any particular speed?

A. Can I stop in time to avoid an accident? The Highway Code says 'Drive at a speed that will allow you to stop well within the distance you can see to be clear' *Rule 57 Stopping Distances*

Q You should always drive at the maximum permitted speed limit for the area you are in. True or false?

A. False. Any speed limit only means it is the maximum permitted and does not necesssarily mean that it is safe to travel at that speed. I would drive at a speed within the limit but dictated by the road, weather and traffic conditions prevailing at the time. *Rule 56*

Q Other than on a motorway, what is the speed limit when you see street lighting? 1. 30mph. 2. 30mph unless signs show otherwise. 3. 40mph.

A. 2. *Rule 54*

TIP: *Very often main roads on the boundaries of towns have a 40mph speed limit. If you are driving at this speed for a while and begin to wonder whether you have missed the 30mph sign some way back, look for the little 40 signs. They are placed, as a reminder, on every third or fourth lamp post, when in a 40mph limit zone. If there are none present, you are in a 30mph limit and should slow down straight away.*

Q Assuming you are a car driver, what speed limits apply to you when on the following types of roads, when 1) towing a trailer or 2) caravan? 1. Roads in built up areas. 2. Single carriageways. 3. Dual-carriageways. 4 Two lane motorways. 5. Three lane motorways.

A. 1. 30 and 30. 2. 60 and 50. 3. 70 and 60. 4. 70 and 60. 5. 70 and 60.
Highway Code Speed Limits Table page 53

25
Stopping Distances

 Q How is the overall stopping distance broken down? 1. Into thinking distance and braking distance. 2. Into thinking, reacting and braking distance.

A. 1.

Q   What is meant by 'thinking distance'?

A. Thinking distance is the extent to which my car moves along the road during the time that it takes me to recognise, process and react to any danger and apply the brakes.

Q   On what approximate period of time is the thinking distance based, and what sort of things are likely to make this period longer? 1. Roughly 0.5 of a second. 2. Just about 1.2 seconds. 3. Nearly 0.7 of a second.

A. 3. Though this would be longer if I were distracted by such things as children, scenery, fiddling with the radio, dazzle, smoking, etc.

Q   What is meant by 'braking distance'?

A. Braking distance is the extent to which my car moves along the road between the time that the brakes 'bite' and when the car stops.

Q   What is meant by 'overall stopping distance'? 1. Thinking distance minus braking distance. 2. Thinking distance plus braking distance. 3. Thinking distance multiplied by braking distance.

A. 2. Therefore overall stopping distance is equal to the time it takes me to think about it and the actual time it takes to stop.   *Highway Code page 15*

Q   What is the thinking distance equivalent, in feet, compared to mph? 1. 10ft to 1mph. 2. 3ft to 1mph. 3. 1ft to 1mph.

A. 3.

Q   So what is the thinking distance for 20, 30, 40, 50, 60 and 70 miles per hour?

A. 20ft, 30ft, 40ft, 50ft, 60ft and 70ft respectively.

FACT: *In metric terms, the thinking distance in metres is: 6m, 9m, 12m, 15m, 18m and 21m respectively.*

FACT: *When it comes to judging speed it is often helpful to think of a vehicle as travelling in ft/second instead of miles/ hour. To work this out is a fairly simple matter.*
  Take 30mph and multiply it by the number of feet in 1 mile (5280).
  30 × 5280 = 158400ft/hour
  Divide by 60 = 2640ft/min
  Divide by 60 = 44ft/second
Using this, 20mph = 29ft/second, 30mph = 44ft/second, 40mph = 59ft/second, 50mph = 73ft/second, 60mph = 88ft/ second, 70mph = 103ft/second.
  If all of this sounds hard work and you quickly want to work out your approximate speed in ft/seconds, just multiply your own speed in mph by 1.5. It's near enough. Incidentally, this is where the 0.7 second thinking distance figure comes from 0.7 second × 44ft/second = 30.8ft (your approximate thinking distance at 30mph).

 Assuming good conditions, what is the overall stopping distance for a car at the following speed? Choose ft, metres or both. 20mph, 30mph, 40mph, 50mph, 60mph and 70mph.

  A. 40ft, 75ft, 120ft, 175ft, 240ft, 315ft (12m, 23m, 36m, 53m, 73m, 96m) *Highway Code page 15*

TIP: *If you got the last question right, it is a simple matter to work out the actual braking distance. Take away the thinking distance at a rate of 1ft for each mph. Therefore the braking distances are: 20ft, 45ft, 80ft, 125ft, 180ft and 245ft respectively (6m, 14m, 24m, 38m, 55m and 75m).* Rule 57

 Every time the speed of your car is doubled the braking distance is trebled. True or false?

  A. False. According to these figures if I double the speed of my car the braking distance is quadrupled.

Q What distance gap is it reasonable to leave between yourself and the car in front, in good conditions? 1. 1ft for each mph of your speed. 2. 1m for each mph of your speed. 3. 1.5m for each mph of your speed.

A. 2.

Q What time gap does the Highway Code suggest should be the minimum between yourself and the car in front, in good conditions? 1. Two seconds. 2. One second. 3. Three seconds.

A. 1. It is called the two second rule. *Rule 57*

TIP: *Try this when you are on the road and the car in front is travelling at approximately the same speed as yourself. When the leading car passes a sign, or gate post, start counting slowly, 'one second, two seconds'. Have you passed the marker at 'one second, t____'? If so, you are too close. Did you get to three seconds? If so, you are allowing yourself a very reasonable amount of room. Good for you.*

TIP: *This is when you can use your ft per second calculation. Because, quite honestly, just being able to repeat overall stopping distances is next to useless if you are unable to benefit from the information by putting it into practice while driving. Imagine you and the car in front are travelling at 50mph. You should leave a gap of 50m (it used to be 50 yards so we'll call it 150ft). At 50mph your speed in ft/second is 73ft/second. In two seconds you will cover 146ft, almost the 150ft needed. If you do this regularly at different speeds and picture the distance in your mind, you will find it much easier to judge distances even when you're not moving, such as when deciding to pull out at junctions, etc.*

SUMMARY: *How does all this work on the road?*

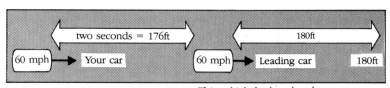

This vehicle brakes sharply

The driver in front of you suddenly brakes sharply. While the driver has been covering thinking distance you don't know what's going to happen because his brake lights don't show until this is over. So, as far as you are concerned, the driver pulls up in 180ft (the braking distance). If you see the brake lights, but only take action after one second of thinking, you will have travelled 268ft before you can stop (88ft at 88ft/second + braking distance of 180ft). How much room have you got left.

176ft gap + 180ft (leading car braking distance) = 356ft.

356ft − 268ft (your overall stopping distance) = 88ft. Even though you have stopped safely, you only have a gap of 88ft left after an initial two second gap of 176ft. Imagine if you were tired, ill or had a couple of drinks at lunchtime. How much room would you have had left then? Surprising isn't it?

Now, suppose the car in front just ran into a stationary car and follows through, pushing it forward 30ft, before coming to rest in your path. You notice the collision as it happens and react within 0.5 of a second. Would you be able to stop in time? Let's see.

176ft gap + 30ft = 206ft. Minus your overall stopping distance of 224ft (44ft at 88ft/sec + 180ft). You overlap with the accident by 18ft, on paper, but because you will also be involved, the impact will not let you cover the last 18ft.

This leads to another question. IS A TWO SECOND GAP ENOUGH? For the most part, probably yes, though it should be doubled, at least, in bad driving conditions. However, in normal conditions if you regularly count to three seconds, leave it.   Rule 57

 All this talk of good roads and dry weather in Britain is a bit optimistic. What happens to overall stopping distances when it's raining and frosty?

A. Braking distances are at least doubled in wet weather, so I should leave a far larger gap between me and the car in front. At least double the one metre rule to two metres and at least double the two second rule to four seconds.

Rule 57

 What conditions would increase the stopping distances besides rain and ice?

A. Inefficient brakes, poor quality or worn tyres and tired drivers.

131

Q In good conditions when travelling at 70mph it should take around 315ft to stop, but if you suddenly came upon a slippery or icy road, it might take you: 1. Up to three times further? 2. Up to seven times further? 3. Up to ten times further?

A. 3.

  Why is this?

A. Because when the roads are slippery or covered in ice, I cannot use much pressure on the brakes before they lock up. I must spread out the braking over a much greater distance.

  When travelling at 50mph on a wet road, it is unlikely that you will be able to stop in a distance less than: 1. 350 yards? 2. 300ft? 3. 275ft?

A. 2. 300ft or 50ft + (125ft × 2).

Q When on a slippery or icy road at 30mph and wishing to pull up at the side of a road or at a junction, how far away should you begin gentle braking? 1. 450ft. 2. 300ft. 3. 150ft.

A. 1. 45 × 10, because it can take me up to 10 times longer to stop in these conditions.

Q The driver behind has never heard of the two second rule and is hitching a ride on your rear bumper. What should you do about it? Give reasons for your answer, for and against. 1. Fume, but do nothing. 2. Brake sharply. 3. Speed up to get away from the car. 4. Hang back from the car in front.

A. 4 is the correct answer, but let me say first why I didn't choose the others. If I get angry, I am likely to make a mistake myself. If I brake sharply, I will cause an accident because there is no way the other driver could stop in time. If I speed up, I will be putting myself at greater risk because the other driver will probably speed up too and if there is a car in front of me, I may get too close to it. On the other hand, if I drop back from the car in front, I am not only giving the car behind a space if I am overtaken, but if I need to stop I can spread out my braking, giving myself and the other drivers a chance.

26

Traffic Signs

Q Traffic signs can be circular, triangular or rectangular. Choose the correct meaning?
   Circles give orders, warnings or information?
   Triangles give information, orders or warnings?
   Rectangles give warnings, information or orders?

A. Most circles give orders. Triangles mostly give warnings. Rectangles usually give information.
                                    See Highway Code pages 58-60

Q What is the difference between red circular signs and blue circular signs?

A. Red circles are mostly prohibitive, while blue circles give positive instruction.   *Rule 44*

Q Define the differences.

A. Prohibitive red circles tell me what I *must not* do. Positive blue circles tell me what I *must* do.

Q What is a red-edged triangular sign trying to do?

A. Give me a warning of a possible hazard ahead. I must be prepared to slow down and drive carefully.

Two of the red signs which give orders, and are encountered often, are not circular to possess added prominence. Which two? 1. A school crossing patrol. 2. A Stop sign. 3. A no entry sign. 4. A Give Way sign.

A. 2 and 4. The octagonal Stop sign and the upside-down triangular Give Way sign.

Signs Giving Orders — Prohibitive and Positive

 What are the correct meanings of these signs?

A. 1. No entry for vehicular traffic. 2. No vehicles. 3. No motor vehicles. 4. All motor vehicles except motor cycles without sidecars prohibited. 5. No vehicles carrying explosives. 6. Ahead only.

Warning Signs

Q Do you know the meaning of these signs? What is the significance of the thicker line?

A. 1. T-junction. 2. Crossroads. 3. Side road. 4. Staggered junction. The thicker line indicates the road with priority through the junction (the side roads will have the Give Way lines).

Q Why are there two signs almost the same and what do they mean? Why are the lines the same size?

1   2

A. The signs mean, traffic merging from two roads into one. 1. From the left. 2. From the right. The road I am on is middle bottom and I am coming upon another road which will merge with me with equal priority, hence the lines of equal thickness.

Q What type of road would you be on if you saw this sign? What does it mean?

A. I would be travelling down a one way street and approaching a junction at which two way traffic crosses in front of me.

Q You could see either of these signs in numerous places along the road. What do they mean?

1   2

A. 1. Road narrows on right (left if symbol reversed). 2. Road narrows on both sides.

Q What does sign 1 (white on blue with red bars) mean? Would you be likely to see sign 2 at the same time?

1   2

A. 1 means no through road. 2 may be included if the road runs out and becomes a mud track further down, but it may also be found in other places where the road is very narrow or badly damaged.

Q Explain 1 (black on white with red bar), 2 (black on yellow with red bar) and 3 (white and red on blue). Why is 3 different from the others?

1   2   3

A. 1 is a three lane carriageway which shortly becomes two lanes. Traffic in the left lane will leave at the next exit on the left. If I want to stay on the same road or turn right I must select the correct lane. 2 is a temporary road sign, showing a right lane closure (road works perhaps). I must keep left in the other available lanes. 3 is nothing to do with available lanes, but means that I have priority over vehicles from the opposite direction, perhaps at a narrow bridge or through a short tunnel.

27

Overtaking

Q The following points of procedure are the ones to use before performing any overtaking manoeuvre. Can you place them in the correct order?

(a) Change gear now if necessary and accelerate. Pull out in a smoothly guided line leaving plenty of room between vehicles. Overtake quickly and confidently.

(b) Check the road ahead and make sure it is clear for a great enough distance.

(c) Ask yourself, 'Is this manoeuvre really necessary?' If so, 'Is it safe to overtake here?'.

(d) Signal in good time before you start the move. This will inform the driver behind, anyone coming towards you in the distance, and the vehicle in front (if the driver is using his mirror).

(e) Check your road position. Are you too far away so that you will spend too much time on the wrong side, or are you too close, restricting your field of vision?

(f) Ask, 'Do I have enough speed in reserve?' Can you overtake without breaking the speed limit for the road you are on? Do you need to change down a gear?

(g) Use your rear view mirror and offside wing mirror, check what's going on behind.

(h) When passed, check that you have cleared the vehicle before pulling back into the left, by the use of interior and nearside wing mirrors.

(i) Check your speed relative to the vehicle in front.

A. 1 — (c). 2 — (e). 3 — (i). 4 — (f). 5 — (b). 6 — (g). 7 — (d). 8 — Rule 100. 9 — (h) Rule 100.

Nobody ever said overtaking was easy. How did you fare?
Rule 99

TIP: *If you need to abandon the procedure at any time and cancel the manoeuvre, start again. Never take up the sequence from where you left off, because, even after a few seconds the distance you have travelled will be quite considerable and the situation will be completely different.*

Q What does this sign mean? 1. Overtake only if your car is red. 2. No overtaking. 3. Overtake with caution because red means danger.

A. 2.

Q What is the cardinal rule to remember about overtaking? 1. If in doubt — do not overtake. 2. If in doubt — overtake anyway, but be quick. 3. If in doubt — good observation will keep you safe.

A. 1.   *Rule 106*

NOTE: *Overtaking puts you at greater risk even if you do everything 'by the book', because you can never be absolutely sure what the other driver is going to do next. You can also be at risk when you are the driver being overtaken, and for the same reason. The following points are to help you decide, when to, when not to, and what to do about being passed, in an overtaking situation. Remember, overtaking is a major cause of injury and death on the roads.*

Q There are many places where you should *never* overtake. How many can you think of?

A. 1. Where I would have to cross or straddle unbroken double white lines, or wherever there are double white lines and the one nearest me is unbroken. 2. Within the zig-zag area on approach to a Zebra crossing. 3. Following a no overtaking sign and anywhere within the restriction area. 4. Near a corner or bend in the road. 5. Near a hump-back bridge. 6. At the brow of a hill. 7. Near a Pelican crossing. 8. On approach to traffic lights. 9. At a road junction. 10. Where there is an island. 11. At a level crossing. 12. Where the road narrows. 13. Where there is only room if I drive on the lane dividing diagonal stripes or chevrons. 14. Where I would force another driver to swerve or brake hard.   *Rule 106*

Q What conditions make it particularly dangerous to overtake and why?

A. At dusk, at night and when it is foggy, misty or the roads are icy. It is more difficult to judge speed and distance and I will require more room to brake in adverse conditions should anyone of us make a mistake.   *Rule 99*

What should you do about overtaking motor cycles, pedal cycles or horse riders, and when are they at greatest risk?

A. I should leave them plenty of room. Cyclists may wobble or swerve in front of me in poor road or weather conditions and horses have an odd habit of walking sideways, perhaps trying to find their balance. Any of these riders are at greater risk if I overtake them immediately before I turn left. I would therefore hang back and pass behind them.   *Rule 101*

When being overtaken by another driver, what are your responsibilities? Choose those you think are correct. 1. Do not increase your speed. 2. Accelerate gently. 3. Slow down if necessary. 4. Sound your horn. 5. Allow the vehicle to pass. 6. Pull out if the driver passes too close. 7. Let the vehicle into your own safety gap if in danger. 8. Once a vehicle pulls in front reassess the gap between yourself and *that* vehicle by dropping back if necessary.

A. 1, 3, 5, 7 and 8 are correct.   *Rule 104*

Why should you be careful when overtaking buses, coaches, milk floats, fruit vans, ice cream vans and mobile library lorries, parked at the side of the road?

A. Because some people, especially children, are far more interested in their purchases to worry about traffic and may walk out into the road in front of me. I would therefore leave plenty of room between myself and the stationary vehicles, slow down and be prepared to stop.   *Rule 67*

For what other reason should you be careful when overtaking stationary vehicles and what should you look for?

A. Because at some point all vehicles will move off again. Local delivery vehicles may only move a few yards and often the driver is more interested in his next stop than in passing traffic. I must look out for anyone sitting in the driver's seat.

Q Are you allowed to break the speed limit when overtaking? 1. Yes. 2. No. 3. Only in an emergency. 4. When in danger from other traffic.

A. 2. I must never overtake if I will put myself in danger.

Q You're driving along a two lane road and in the distance an approaching vehicle comes over to your lane to overtake. How do you react and warn of your presence? 1. Sound your horn loudly. 2. Do nothing until you get closer. 3. Flash your headlamps and slow down. 4. Hope that the driver makes it before you get there.

A. 3. Because that's what flashing headlights means.
Rule 135

Q How may you tell the driver in front that you are about to overtake?

A. Again I can quickly flash my headlights so that the driver's attention is brought to my indicator signal.
Rule 135

Q Before overtaking a parked vehicle on your side of the road, to whom should you give priority?

A. Anyone coming towards me on the other side whose lane I intend to use when passing.   *Rule 105*

Q Under what circumstances are you allowed to overtake on the left?
1. When the vehicle in front shows an intention to turn right.
2. When the vehicle in front is turning right, you can pass in the left hand bus lane at any time.
3. When you want to turn left at a junction.
4. When you are in the left lane and traffic is moving slowly in queues.

---

5. On a dual-carriageway.
6. In a one way street.
7. When in the left lane on a motorway and intending to leave by the next exit road.
8. When in a left turn filtering lane.
9. When in the right lane which is moving slower than the left, and I want to get away faster.
10. Anytime, if you can do so safely.

A. 1. Yes. 2. No. 3. Yes. 4. Yes. 5. No. 6. Yes. 7. No. 8. Yes. 9. No (Rule 103). 10. No. *Rule 102*

TIP: *The majority of overtaking accidents occur when fast traffic is approaching behind and a driver pulls out in front of it. You must be especially careful on fast roads, where vehicles may be coming toward you much more quickly than you think. Check the lane behind is clear for a considerable distance.*

Rule 99

Q What is wrong with this overtaking manoeuvre? Who could overtake correctly?

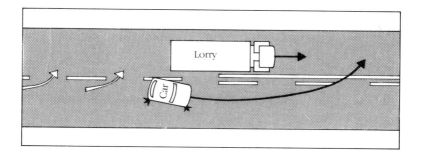

A. The driver of the car should never have started this overtaking manoeuvre because he can't get back on his own side of the road before reaching the solid white line. If the road were clear, a driver coming from the opposite direction may cross the line to overtake, because the other side is painted with broken dashes. *Rule 85*

Q When travelling uphill where there are three lanes, you may see road markings like this. What do the lines mean and why is there a solid white line on the right? Surely vehicles going downhill can also overtake, can't they?

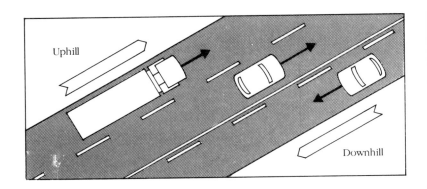

Uphill

Downhill

A. The lines are lane markings and show that there are two lanes uphill and one lane downhill. This helps me overtake slower moving vehicles when travelling uphill. The vehicles going downhill can overtake if the road is clear, as dictated by the broken white line, but priority should be given to uphill traffic. The solid line isn't for downhill traffic at all, but is to tell me when going uphill that there is only one lane available for overtaking. I must not cross into the third lane.

28

Reversing

Q Before reversing, what precautions should you take? 1. Look to see if the reversing lights are working. 2. Check that it's completely clear behind you. 3. Unfasten your seat belt.

A. 2. *Rule 129*

NOTE: *Pay particular attention to the presence of children, who may be hidden from your view, below the rear window, perhaps sitting on the kerb edge.*

Q If you cannot see, before reversing you should: 1. Sound your horn in a series of taps? 2. Put on your hazard warning lights? 3. Get someone to help guide you? 4. Move forward a bit, so you can see what was previously hidden? 5. Get out and have a look?

A. 3 and/or 5. Rule 117

Q When reversing, what points are relevant to the manoeuvre? 1. Adjust your seating position. 2. Look all around everywhere. 3. Signal with an indicator. 4. Keep the vehicle moving slowly. 5. Ignore other traffic unless you swing into the wrong lane. 6. Show consideration to other road users and give way when necessary. 7. Keep the vehicle and its position on the road under control. 8. Keep right in tight to the kerb.

A. 1, 2, 4, 6 and 7.

Q Into which of the following are you not allowed to reverse? 1. From a side road into a main road. 2. Into your driveway. 3. From a main road into a side road. 4. Into a parking space.

A. 1. Although if you want to turn round and decide to reverse from a main road into a side road, first check that the roads aren't narrow or busy, so that you don't cause traffic chaos or an accident. *Rule 130*

Q Where is the 'blind area' in picture *A.* and what can you do to overcome it? Imagine yourself reversing around the corner.

A. The rear pillars and eye level to ground level below rear of window.

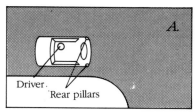
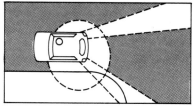

Eye level to ground
level below rear of window

Because of these blind spot areas I would continue a sequence of good observations all the way around the corner. *Rule 129*

FACT: *You should never reverse on a motorway.*

143

Q How far are you allowed to reverse in one move? 1. 10m. 2. As far as you like if your forward gears are smashed. 3. Not more than necessary to complete a reasonable manoeuvre. 4. 25m. 5. Half a mile.

A. 3. *Rule 129*

Q The rules are that you can remove your seat belt when reversing. Is this true or false?

A. True. This should only be necessary if the belt is uncomfortable or restrictive when you are looking to the rear. Most seat belts are now inertia reel and will 'give' if pulled on gently, allowing greater freedom of movement, so that it remains comfortable. Besides, you may forget to put it back on afterwards.

Q What are reversing lights for and how should they be wired in?

A. They are to help me see when reversing in the dark. During the day they tell other drivers, coming up behind me, that I have selected reverse gear and am preparing to move back when they have gone past. Reversing lights should be wired into a switch in the gearbox so that they can be turned on only when in reverse gear. Otherwise, if I use a manual switch on the dashboard, it should be accompanied by a warning light, so that I remember to turn the lights off again afterwards.

NOTE: *You will find more tips on reversing in Chapter 48 on manoeuvring.*

29
Night Driving

Q What is the main danger when driving at night?

A. I can't see as far as I can during the daytime, and information that was previously available is no longer readily apparent. Also, it becomes more difficult to judge the speed of approaching vehicles when all I can see is their lights.

Q How would you adjust your car and your driving to suit night driving? 1. Fit extra spotlights. 2. Make proper use of your car lights. 3. Wear sunglasses to cut out glare. 4. Drive faster to get the adrenalin flowing and make yourself more alert. 5. Drive at a speed relevant to the conditions. 6. Driver slower generally. 7. Stare at approaching cars so that you drive in a straight line. 8. Keep your eyes on your own side of the road in order that you aren't drawn towards the lights of approaching cars.

A. 2, 5, 6 and 8.

Q How can you tell if you are driving too fast at night. 1. If you have several 'near misses' in rapid succession. 2. If you cannot stop within the range of your headlights. 3. If you cannot stop within twice the range of your headlights.

A. 2. I make sure that I can stop well within the distance I can see ahead (either on dipped or main beam).

Rule 57

TIP: *Try this sometime on an unlit road, when it is safe. Drive along noting your speed and pick an object which suddenly comes into your lights. Attempt to stop before you get there. Try this on dipped headlights as well, you may be surprised to find the object is behind you. Use main beam on unlit roads when you can, only dipping them when you would otherwise dazzle another driver in front of you or the driver coming towards you.*

Q What part of your car should be particularly clean when driving at night and why? 1. The interior. 2. The ashtray. 3. The windscreen. 4. The bodywork.

A. The windscreen, but I shouldn't forget the other windows. Dust, mud, grease and scratches cause light to scatter and can 'white out' the window during the times that another's lights shine at me.

Q When should you dip your main beam headlights when driving at night? 1. When you enter a built up area with street lights. 2. If you want to see the stars more clearly. 3. If you come up behind another vehicle on your side. 4. When you meet another vehicle coming towards you. 5. When you have been overtaken by another car.

A. 1, 3, 4 and 5. *Rules 131 & 132*

Q How can you cause a nuisance to drivers in front when driving at night?

A. First, if I don't dip my main beam. I will blind the driver through the rear view mirror and both the side mirrors. Secondly, if I drive too close on dipped beam the same thing will apply so I would keep well back. *Rule 132*

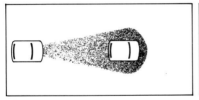

WRONG!

RIGHT

Q What optical equipment is available to aid night driving? 1. Sunglasses. 2. Night driving spectacles. 3. Ski goggles. 4. Tinted helmet visors. 5. Spray on tinting material. 6. None of these. 7. All of these?

A. 6. *Rule 35*

NOTE: *Drivers should not use tinted optical equipment of any kind, either at night or during periods of poor daytime visibility.*
Rule 35
However, if you need to wear glasses or contact lenses to meet the official eyesight standard, then you must do so, as to drive without them is an offence. *Rule 34*

30

Driving in Adverse Conditions

Adverse conditions usually mean the prevailing weather during the time you are on the road. It really is quite frightening to find yourself unable to see the road ahead after suddenly driving into an area of thick fog, especially after dark. The main thing is, don't panic, but act quickly. The following is a series of helpful hints and rules for driving in such conditions.

Fog

 How may points can you think of that would be relevant when driving in fog? Think of speed, distance and lights.

A. 1. Check my mirror and slow down. 2. I must keep a safe distance from the car in front. 3. I must always be able to pull up within my range of vision. 4. I wouldn't hang on to someone else's tail lights. 5. I would watch my speed and check it regularly. 6. I must not accelerate to increase the gap between me and the vehicle behind. 7. If I am driving a heavy vehicle I need longer to stop or slow down. 8. I would observe all warning signs. 9. I need to use my dipped headlights so that I can see and be seen (Rule 131). 10. I can use rear fog lamps in really thick fog (Rule 133). 11. I should use my demisters and windscreen wipers. 12. The journey can be made safer if I clean my lights, windows and reflectors regularly. 13. I must remember fog can be patchy and refrain from accelerating between patches. 14. In bad fog, I would only travel if the journey was important and also allow plenty of time for it.

Rule 58

 What is wrong with following the tail lights of another vehicle in thick fog? After all, you may think that if the driver in front is okay, you are too.

A. 1. No. I am not necessarily okay. If the driver in front gets into trouble, I may be driving into a disaster. 2. If the fog gets thicker I can run into the rear of the car in front. 3. I may encourage the drive to go faster to get away from me. 4. The driver in front may be driving too close to the centre line, perhaps using it as a guide, so we may both encounter traffic from the opposite direction doing the same. 5. Relying on someone else to guide the way instills a false sense of security.

 You want to turn right into a side road but you must stop and wait because in the fog you see headlights coming toward you. What should you do to prevent anyone hitting you from behind? 1. Use hazard warning lights. 2. Use arm signals as well as the indicator. 3. Keep your foot on the brake pedal so your rear lights are more distinct.

A. 3. But I mustn't forget to keep my right indicator on.

 Where is it most dangerous to park in the fog?

A. On the road. *Rule 144*

 It is safer to find an off road parking place, but if you must park on the road in fog, what precautions must you take? 1. Leave sidelights switched on. 2. Put hazard lights on. 3. Leave the interior light on. 4. Leave the left indicator flashing.

A. 1. I must also park facing in the direction of the traffic flow. *Rules 142 & 144*

 Why is fog on a motorway particularly hazardous? 1. It is patchy. 2. Motorways make you feel you are travelling slowly. 3. Fog presents no particular problems. 4. Motorway signs may be missed. 5. Some drivers don't seem to take much notice. 6. Some drivers think speeding up between patches is safe if their lights are on. 7. Some drivers ignore recommended speed limits.

A. 1, 2, 4, 5, 6 and 7.

TIP: *Always allow plenty of time for your journey because, whether on a motorway or an ordinary road, it is easy to miss your turning when the signs are obscured by fog. You may therefore take much longer to reach your destination if you use unfamiliar roads.*

Snow

 You are driving in snow and have to pull up at a junction. The road clears and you try to pull away, but the wheels spin. What have you done wrong and what can you do about it?

A. Firstly, I probably used too high revs on the engine as the clutch plates came together, reducing the chance of the wheels to grip the snowy covering. If I had anticipated this, I could have chosen a higher gear, such as second gear, to pull away. *Rules 61 & 62*

NOTE: *You will need more revs to pull away in second gear so that the engine doesn't stall. However, the higher gear reduces the amount of turning on the drive wheels for the same amount of work done by the engine, the result being that the wheels turn slower, increasing the grip.*

TIP: *If your drive wheels spin on snow or ice, when pulling away or while on the move, stop this as quickly as possible by coming off the accelerator (not stamping on the brake). Never let the wheels continue to spin in the hope of burning your way through the ice, down to the road surface, to get some grip. It doesn't work. Instead the vehicle will start to slide sideways, usually with the camber of the road, but often into the path of oncoming vehicles which, like you, will have great difficulty stopping.* *Rule 61*

 How should you negotiate a snow covered hill? Tick one. 1. Keep the engine revs as high as possible. 2. Change down into first gear at the bottom. 3. Take some hay to put under the wheels if you get stuck. 4. Drive steadily and try to keep moving. 5. Drive slowly and keep stopping to clean tyre thread. 6. Drive up as quickly as possible.

A. 4.

Ice

Q What allowances should you make when braking in wet or icy roads?

A. I would be driving slower in the first place so this should give me more time to use the brake effectively. I would avoid fierce braking. Instead, I should spread the braking over a longer distance so that I don't skid.

Q How much distance should you leave between yourself and the car in front when compared to dry conditions? 1. At least the same distance. 2. At least twice the distance. 3. At least four times the distance.

A. 2. I should normally leave at least one metre for each mph of speed and double this to two metres, at least. More is better. *Rule 57*

FACT: *Stopping on icy roads can require up to ten times the stopping distances normal on dry roads. Ice isn't the only problem. At other times of the year their are other risks. Mud at any time, slimy leaves in the autumn, rain, puddles and showers all require you to leave yourself far more stopping distance than normal.*

Q How can you reduce the risk of skidding on icy roads? 1. Use the highest suitable gear for your speed. 2. Drive in second gear regardless of speed. 3. Switch on your lights. 4. Use a low gear.

A. 1. A higher gear reduces the response at the wheels after movement of the accelerator pedal. *Rule 60*

Rain and Flooding

Q If the roads have been thoroughly dried out after several weeks of fine weather, when will they be most slippery? 1. After several hours of continuous rain. 2. After it stops raining. 3. Just after it starts raining.

A. 3.

Before driving through a flooded road what should you do first?

A. I must check how deep the water is before going in and look out for a depth gauge if the area is flooded regularly.

 After you have driven through the flood, what should you check immediately? 1. Your lights still work. 2. Your brakes. 3. Water in the ignition system. 4. Water in the exhaust pipe.

A. 2.

TIP: *Drive through a flood slowly in first gear and slip the clutch to keep the revs high, but your speed down. To dry your brakes, drive slowly and lightly press the brake pedal with your left foot for a short distance, after emerging.*

 What do these signs mean?

1

2

A. 1. A worded warning sign. 2. Found after a ford or before descending a steep hill. Both can be warning of a flood.

SUMMARY: *Remember to drive more slowly in bad weather. Brakes are unlikely to get you out of trouble. They are far more likely to make a bad situation worse.* Rule 59

31
Alcohol, Drugs,
Illness and Tiredness

FACT: *Everyone knows that consuming alcohol before driving*

seriously affects judgement. The levels of alcohol a driver must by law not exceed are:
35 microgrammes of alcohol per 100 millilitres of breath.
80 milligrammes of alcohol per 100 millilitres of blood.
107 milligrammes of alcohol per 100 millilitres of urine.
                            Rule 39 and The Road User and the Law

---

Q   How much alcohol are these amounts equivalent to? 1. One pint of beer. 2. One pint + two shorts. 3. The amount varies from person to person. 4. Three glasses of wine. 5. None of these?

A.   For some people even small amounts of alcohol have a large intoxicating effect, so answer 3 is most appropriate.

NOTE: *The law does not state that you are sober up to these levels. If you are unsure DO NOT DRINK AND DRIVE.*
                                                         Rule 39

 Why should you not drive or start a journey: 1. When under the influence of alcohol? 2. When taking medication? 3. When you are ill? 4. When you are tired?

A.   1. Alcohol reduces co-ordination, increases reaction time and impairs judgement of speed, distance and risk, reduces the eyes' ability to focus and cope with glare, while inspiring a false sense of confidence. You actually *think* you're fit to drive. 2. Many medicines and tablets have a similar effect to alcohol. Containers and bottles should contain a warning about driving and operating machinery if the contents have a stupefying effect. If there is any doubt I should consult my doctor or pharmacist. 3. Illness is usually associated with irritability, exhaustion and lack of awareness. Feelings which are exacerbated by medication. 4. Tiredness can cause serious accidents because of impaired judgement and delayed reaction time. There is also a risk of falling asleep at the wheel.   *Rules 33 & 39*

Q   What proportion of accident victims killed on the roads are related to the consumption of alcohol? 1. 10%. 2. 25%. 3. 33%?

A.   3. MoT statistics state that one third of all persons killed on the road are over the legal limit for alcohol.

Q What is likely to happen if you are stopped by the police and shown to be over the legal limit for alcohol?

A. First I will be arrested and taken to the police station. Then another analysis will be carried out. I could be locked up while identification checks are made. If the second analysis proves positive I will be charged and summoned to appear in court. Upon appearance I will lose my licence (perhaps for several years) and receive a heavy fine or imprisonment. If any damage or death has been caused other charges will result.

Q What is the safest course as far as alcohol is concerned?

A. Don't drink alcohol if I intend to drive.

Q If you feel tired or sleepy during a long drive what should you do? 1. Put the car on automatic. 2. Open the window. 3. Smoke a cigarette. 4. Put your lights on.

A. 2. I should get plenty of fresh air and pull in somewhere safe to rest for a while.   *Rules 31 & 32*

TIP: *Changing your field of view, that is, keeping your eyes moving, helps keep you alert and reduces eye strain. Look well ahead, mid range and near, to the sides and at your instruments and mirrors.*

32
Car Telephones and CB Microphones

Q You own a car telephone, CB or dictation recorder. Which of the following apply to the use of these devices? 1. Only use in an emergency. 2. Only use while moving in an emergency. 3. Never stop on the hard shoulder of a motorway to make or receive a call. 4. Never stop at the roadside to make or receive a call. 5. Use a fixed, neckslung or clip-on microphone when it does not distract attention from the road. 6. Pull into the service area, or off at the next junction of a motorway to make calls. 7. Use anywhere when broken down to call for assistance. 8. Only take calls if a passenger answers the phone and says 'It's for you'.

A. 2, 3, 5, 6 and 7.

FACT: *The number of crash victims found clutching CB microphones and telephones is alarmingly high. For your own safety, don't use telephone handsets or microphones while your car is moving. If a call comes through and you have passengers, let them deal with it. If you are on your own, pull over somewhere safe before answering or making that call or recording a message.* Rule 43

33
Lighting the Way

Sidelights, Dipped Headlamps, Main Beam Headlamps

Q What are your responsibilities as far as the lights on your car are concerned? There are several points.

A. It is my responsibility to make sure the lights are clean, front and rear, that they are all working and are correctly adjusted. Also that I use them as and when it becomes necessary. *Rules 28 & 131*

TIP: *If you are driving at night with dipped headlights and find that irate drivers keep flashing their headlights at you, suspect the adjustment of your lights. The screws that control this can wobble loose with vibration and time. If you can't adjust them yourself, take the car to an MOT garage where the mechanic has the means to test and rectify the problem in a few minutes. Remember also that badly adjusted headlamps can dazzle the driver of the car ahead of you, on your side.*

Q When must you switch on your headlights in the evening?

A. At lighting up time. However, if the sky is full of dark clouds, visibility can drop considerably before the street lamps come on, so I would use my lights earlier if necessary.   *Rule 131*

 Which of the following situations would cause you to use dipped headlights during the daytime? 1. Light rain. 2. Heavy rain. 3. Fog. 4. A crowded street. 5. Snow. 6. Thrown up spray. 7. Mist.

A. 2, 3, 5 and 7. For example, when visibility is reduced to less than 100m.   *Rule 131*

TIP: *When driving in a multi-storey car park, where the lighting is usually minimal, use your sidelights until you have found somewhere to park.*

 A police car is approaching slowly with its headlights on. It is broad daylight and you are approaching a bend in the road. What could this mean and what would you do about it?

A. It's likely that the police are escorting an exceptionally wide, long or slow moving vehicle along the road. They are telling me to expect something unusual around the corner and so I would slow down and be prepared to stop if necessary.

TIP: *When replacing broken bulbs of any kind, make sure that you fit the correct size. This usually means the same type of bulb, so check the wattage number on the glass before buying. The brightness should be the same on both sides of the car, so if the glass is broken, check the opposite bulb before replacing.*

 Are you legally allowed to drive your car during the day if the lights aren't working? 1. Yes if the sun is shining. 2. Yes if you're home before dark. 3. No. 4. Only in an emergency.

A. 3. I may drive only if my lamps are working and comply with the regulations.   *The Road User & the Law*

Q When are dipped headlights compulsory at lighting up time? 1. Where there are no street lamps. 2. Where faulty street lamps aren't working. 3. Where street lamps are over 185m (200 yards) apart. 4. On motorways generally. 5. On lighted motorways. 6. On dual-carriageways. 7. In built up areas.

A. I would use dipped headlights for all the situations suggested. *Rules 131 & 132*

Q When should you, and when should you not, use your main beam headlights? 1. During the night. 2. When no vehicles are in front of you. 3. On country roads. 4. On unlit roads between towns. 5. In towns and cities with street lights. 6. When you come upon approaching traffic (Mark yes or no.)

A. 1, 2, 3 and 4 = yes. 5 and 6 = no.

Q When dazzled by the main beam headlights of an oncoming car, what should you do? 1. Look over your shoulder. 2. Shut your eyes for a few seconds. 3. Slow down or stop. 4. Retaliate by flashing your headlamps. 5. Keep your eyes looking left. 6. Keep blinking rapidly.

A. 3 and 5. I must slow down or stop and while doing so keep looking left of the light source as much as possible.

NOTE: *Never flash your lights as both of you will be blinded which can cause a serious accident.* *Rule 132*

Rear Fog Lamps — Eye Level Brake Lamp

Q When should a driver use high intensity rear fog lights? 1. When visibility is seriously reduced to less than 100m. 2. When it is dark or raining. 3. When visibility is reduced to less than 500m. 4. When it is snowing.

A. 1. During times of mist, heavy rain, fog or heavy snow. *Rule 133*

NOTE: *These lights are used to 'punch a hole' into thick fog, so that the car behind can see you when your normal side and brake lights can't cope. If used at any other time, they are far too* *bright and will dazzle the driver behind, perhaps causing an accident.*

TIP: *If you are able, fit yourself an eye level brake light in the back window. They are reputed to reduce rear end collisions by up to 50 per cent and are therefore a very welcome driving aid. It isn't bright enough to dazzle, but does attract immediate attention because it is almost directly in the line of sight of the following driver. It is also separate from the shared light cover of side- and brake lights in many cars. They can be seen by drivers further back when your car brake lights are hidden by the car directly behind. However, it is most important that the light itself is set into a 'cup' and attached directly to the window, as escaping red light will scatter over the back window and reduce your own rear visibility.*

Flashing Headlamps

 When it is felt to be necessary, you may flash your headlamps at another vehicle to: 1. Show your anger at bad driving? 2. Give information about hazards ahead? 3. Say 'Hi' to a friend? 4. Give instructions? 5. Warn of your presence? 6. Let them go first? 7. Tell them to get out of the way? 8. Let the driver know his main beam is dazzling you?

A. Headlamp flashing has only one meaning: 5. To warn of my presence. It has no other official meaning.

Rule 135

 The answer to the previous question was 5, so would it be right to ignore any driver who flashes his headlamps at you after you have become aware of his presence?

A. No, I wouldn't ignore it.

TIP: *Not everyone is aware of the rules for flashing headlamps. If a driver comes around a bend ahead of you flashing his lights, he is obviously trying to tell you something besides 'I am here'. Perhaps there is a herd of cattle or an accident just around the bend. What else can he do to warn others? Certainly don't ignore it, slow down and see. However, don't interpret another's flashing lights as an instruction or an indication of intent, for example, at a junction. What you think the driver is telling you may be wrong and the signal may not even be for* *you. Treat such signals by others carefully and don't rely on them for your own safety. Make sure before you move off.*

 Q How could you interpret Rule 135 when overtaking by day or night?

A. If the driver in front doesn't know what the interior mirror is for and seems to be unaware of my presence, I could flash my lights at him before starting the overtaking manoeuvre. It really must only be a flash or you could blind the driver momentarily. He then becomes aware of my indicator and will witness the manoeuvre, making him less likely to pull out in front of me or change lanes suddenly.

Hazard Warning Lights

 Q If your car is fitted with four way hazard warning lights, under what circumstances are you permitted to use them? 1. When the vehicle is stationary. 2. When you are parked dangerously. 3. When breaking the speed limit. 4. When loading, unloading or making deliveries. 5. When causing a temporary obstruction. 6. When carrying an unbalanced load. 7. When the vehicle is overloaded. 8. When broken down. 9. Any time the vehicle is moving. 10. To avoid an accident.

A. 1, 4, 5 and 8. Be aware that 2, 3, 6 and 7 are illegal anyway. *Rule 134*

Q Can you use your flashing hazard lights during an emergency when travelling along, perhaps to hospital or when late for an appointment, to indicate that you are in a hurry?

A. No. The hazard lights should not be used while the vehicle is in motion. *Rule 134*

NOTE: *The rules have changed slightly in recent times. It has been established that additional use of hazard lights can be beneficial to other road users during times when you need to slow quickly on fast roads, such as motorways or dual-carriageways. If you see an accident ahead or cattle wandering across the road, you can use them briefly to warn others of the danger.*

34

*U*se of the Horn

Q What is the one occasion that you are correct when using the horn of your car? 1. When you are angry. 2. To let others know you are angry. 3. When you spot your friend in the high street. 4. As a warning of your presence. 5. To warn of another's careless driving. 6. When the car in front stalls at the lights. 7. To let a driver turning right pass in front of you.

A. 4. I should only use my horn to warn others of my presence. *Rule 136*

Q A driver pulls out in front of you suddenly and makes you brake sharply. You give the driver a good blast on the horn, because of the danger. Okay?

A. No, even though blowing my horn is the most lenient reprimand I can think of, I would never use it as a rebuke or in anger, only as a warning to others of my presence during normal driving. *Rule 136*

Q It is an offence to sound the horn of your car, in a built up area, between certain times. Which times? 1. 7pm–7am (19.00–07.00). 2. 11.30pm–7am (23.30–07.00). 3. 11pm–7.30am (23.00–07.30). 4. 7am–11.30pm (07.00–23.30).

A. 2. *Rule 136 The Road User & the Law*

FACT: *Sounding your horn when stationary is an offence, except when in danger from another moving vehicle.*
Rule 136

Q Use of the horn gives you right of way in most situations. True or false?

A. False, sounding the horn never gives me right of way. I use it to warn a driver who I think hasn't seen me.

Q If you drive properly you shouldn't need to use your horn very often, but on very narrow country roads with sharp bends and areas of 'dead ground' use of your horn can increase safety to yourself, pedestrians and other drivers coming in the opposite direction. However, this does not relieve you of your responsibilities. What are these?

A. Driving safely and slowing down where necessary.

Q Drivers vary the sounds of their horns depending on whom they wish to warn. Who are the following aimed at? 1. A quick tap. 2. A series of short taps. 3. A longer more emphatic note.

A. A quick tap is enough to warn pedestrians and cyclists who I intend to overtake, without alarming them. A series of short taps will attract the attention of children who are playing near the road and perhaps haven't seen me. A longer more emphatic note attracts the attention of other drivers who are somewhat insulated from sounds outside the car.

35
Animals on the Road and in your Care

Q If you meet animals on the road, what action should you take so as not to frighten them? There are at least five points.

A. I must: 1. Slow down and drive past slowly. 2. Give them plenty of room. 3. Be ready to stop and wait if necessary. 4. Don't sound my horn, and 5. Don't rev the engine.   *Rules 80 & 81*

Q When are you most likely to come upon animals unexpectedly? 1. On a left hand bend. 2. On a right hand bend. 3. On the motorway. 4. Near a dog's home.

A. 1. Animals should be led on the left hand side of the road so I will most likely come upon them unexpectedly after negotiating a left hand bend. **Rule 80**

NOTE: *Be especially careful in the country where herds of cattle or sheep may completely block the road.*

 You are driving up a winding country lane and see someone frantically flagging you down. What is the probable reason?

A. Rule 214 of the Highway Code says that anyone who is herding animals, should, if practical, send someone ahead to warn drivers at bends and the brows of hills.

Q What safety precautions should a horse rider or cattle herder take, by day and by night?

A. Horse riders should wear a hard hat at all times when riding. This is compulsory for children under 14. After sunset, both types of animal handlers should wear light or reflective clothing and carry a light (white to face front and red to the rear) so that I can see them and the size of the herd. **Rules 214, 215, 218 & 219**

Q Horses should be ridden: 1. On the pavement? 2. On the right of the road? 3. On the left of the road?

A. 3. Also, when a rider is leading a second horse, the second horse should be on the left of the rider.

Rule 220

FACT: *It is an offence to ride, lead or drive a horse on the pavement which is set apart for pedestrians.*
Rule 222 & The Road User & the Law

 You notice horse riders ahead of you travelling in your direction down a country road. What should you do about it? 1. Tap lightly on your horn to let them know you are coming. 2. Avoid making unnecessary noise with your engine. 3. Slow down. 4. Get past quickly but safely. 5. Move over as much as you can. 6. Brake firmly. 7. Use your flashing hazard lights.

A. 2, 3 and 5.

Q How can you make sure that your dog doesn't disturb you when driving?

A. Tie it up in the back seat or use a dog guard. Even so I must beware of a sudden bark which may startle me.

Rule 213

 Q You've parked your car and intend taking the dog while you visit friends. It seems rather excited, can you let it out for a run up the road first?

A. Definitely not. The road is a dangerous place even for the most obedient and well behaved dog. First I would attach a lead so that I can keep it under control.

Rules 212 & 213

Q What is the correct meaning of each of these signs?

1   2   3
4   5 6

A. 1. Wild horses or ponies. 2. Accompanied horses crossing the road. 3. Unfenced sheep. 4. Wild animals on the road. 5. Cattle crossing. 6. No horse-drawn vehicles.

NOTE: *Occasionally the cattle sign will have alternate flashing amber lights beneath, for use when cattle are being moved across a road at milking and other times. Remember, too, that new signs have recently been introduced for use during times that other wild animals are on the road in great numbers. A toad in a triangular red edged sign is used near lakes and reservoirs during the spawning season as the animals migrate across country to find water.*

 Q You are driving along a busy street past a row of parked cars and a dog dashes out in front of your car. You must do your best to stop, how would you go about this? 1. Swerve out of the way. 2. Brake hard and then swerve. 3. Brake firmly in a straight line. 4. Neither swerve nor brake.

A. 3. This will depend on the amount of traffic. If you constantly have a good working knowledge of following traffic, you may be able to stop in time without endangering others behind. Otherwise coming off the accelerator quickly may slow you down enough to give the dog a chance.

 If you are involved in an accident which causes you to injure or kill an animal belonging to someone else, you must report it to the police within 24 hours and produce your insurance certificate to the same within seven days. Which of the following animals are covered by this law? 1. Horse. 2. Cat. 3. Hedgehog. 4. Goat. 5. Chicken. 6. Cattle. 7. Deer. 8. Ass. 9. Mule. 10. Badger. 11. Sheep. 12. Goose. 13. Pig. 14. Squirrel. 15. Dog.

A. 1, 4, 6, 8, 9, 11, 13 and 15.

36
Road Works

Road works are a necessary evil, whether it be digging trenches, relaying the surface or just painting on lines. In any event it is very important that a driver keeps an eye open for traffic signals or lights and reduces speed as soon as these are encountered. Never drive close to the edge of a trench as the sides may cave in, taking the car and you with it.

 What do these signs mean?

A. 1. Road works ahead. 2. Change to opposite carriage-way ahead, the sign may also be reversed. 3. Loose chippings.

FACT: *When a road has to be temporarily closed or cordoned off you will see this red and white sign. Perhaps for a street fair or a burst water main.* ■■ ■ ■

Q What is this sign used for (white on red)? 1. Stop at the junction. 2. Stop at the road works. 3. Stop at a level crossing.

A. 2. It is a manually operated road works sign, used when there are no traffic lights and drivers must stop when told to do so. The reverse side (white on green) says 'Go'.

Q What special procedures should you adopt at all road works whether on ordinary roads or on motorways?

A. I would observe the signs, signals and speed limits. Check mirrors, select the appropriate lane early and slow down. Keep a safe distance from the vehicle in front and the men working nearby.   *Rules 147, 148 & 177*

Q Road works often reduce traffic down to one lane, in which case this sign is used (white on blue). What does it mean?

A. Keep left, and, if the symbol is reversed, keep right.

37
Temporary Obstructions

Sometimes it becomes necessary to interrupt the flow of traffic for other forms of transport, which cannot, for various reasons, be expected to stop for us. When this occurs a special set of lights are used, like this (red flashing and amber):

 Q What do the red flashing lights mean and what road markings will you see? 1. Keep going. 2. Don't stop here. 3. Stop. 4. Give way if necessary. (a) A solid white Stop line. (b) A double broken Stop line. (c) A single broken Give Way line.

A. 3 and (a).

FACT: *For the most part these lights will be off altogether so that traffic can flow normally. The steady amber light may precede the flashing red by a few seconds and also means Stop, unless it is unsafe for you to do so.*

Q What sort of places would you expect to see these alternating flashing red lights?

A. At railway level crossings, airfields, below aircraft landing paths which cross the road, lifting or swing bridges, entrances to fire and ambulance stations.

 Q Whilst driving along you notice a very narrow bridge ahead, crossing a river or railway line, and see this sign on your approach (black and red in red circle). What does it mean?

A. I must give priority to vehicles from the opposite direction.

Q   What do these signs mean?

A. 1. Lifting, opening or swing bridge ahead. 2. Low-flying aircraft or sudden aircraft noise.

Q   What should you look for when approaching a low bridge?

A. I should establish that I can get under it with my vehicle, and that a high vehicle from the other side, which needs to use the centre of the bridge for clearance, isn't in the middle of the road.

Q   Other dangers which drivers encounter may involve hold-ups. These have warning signs before the danger area. What are their meanings?

A. 1. Height limit ahead (e.g. low bridge); signs may be in metric or imperial units or both. Width markings (optional) show the available width of headroom available. Unsigned bridges are normally at least 16ft 6ins high in the centre but may be less at the sides. 2. Overhead electric cable. The plate indicates the maximum safe height for vehicles. 3. Risk of falling or fallen rocks. 4. Uneven road. 5. Tunnel ahead. 6. Hump bridge ahead. 7. Quayside or river bank ahead or alongside.

NOTE: *Most of the warning signs will have signs like these to indicate the distance to, and the duration of, the hazard.*

┌─────────┐   ┌─────────┐
│ 1 mile │   │   For   │
└─────────┘   │ 2 miles │
                      └─────────┘

38
Waiting and Parking

Parking can be a touchy subject especially if you inadvertently 'pinch' a space that another driver has claimed for him/herself. Waiting while others are preparing to leave a space can also cause tension between parties. Remember, parking spaces are for everyone and one of the attributes of a good driver is patience. If you don't park for free, you will have hired a space for a set period, whether or not you use all of it. A shortage of parking bays should not be used as an excuse for a fight or to engender bad temper, as this can easily spill out onto the road and your driving will suffer, perhaps resulting in an accident.

 What do these road markings mean?

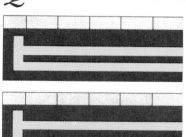

1. No waiting.
2. Park between yellow lines.
3. Only park in the mornings.
4. No parking until after 6pm.
5. (a) Park for 2 minutes only.
   (b) Park for 5 minutes only.
   (c) Park anytime for 20 minutes.

A. All the road markings mean 1. No waiting. However, there may be certain times when parking is allowed. Yellow lines indicate the following:

Double yellow lines — no waiting for at least eight hours between 7am and 7pm on four or more days of the week. The restriction may be in force for longer than the working day, beyond 7pm and before 7am, perhaps a continuous prohibition.

Single yellow line — no waiting for at least eight hours between 7am and 7pm on four or more days of the week.

Broken yellow lines — any other restriction not covered by single or double yellow lines. Waiting is often limited to a certain strict period and/or may be prohibited during certain times of the day, such as rush hours.

 Are you allowed to stop on yellow lines at all?

A. Yes, I am allowed to stop long enough for loading or unloading or to allow passengers to board or alight. I can also park when the plate restrictions run out. *Rule 145*

 There are lots of places where you are not allowed to park, and for a variety of reasons. For example, you may make the road too narrow, you may make it difficult for others to see, pedestrians or traffic could be held up or inconvenienced and you may interrupt the flow of emergency vehicles. How many places can you think of where parking is prohibited?

A. 1. On motorways (except on hard shoulder in an emergency). 2. On clearway carriageways (except in emergency). 3. On urban clearways (during signed times — except for dropping or picking up passengers). 4. In bus lanes (during operative times). 5. In cycle lanes (during operative times). 6. On the carriageway or verge where there are double white lines (even if one is broken), except to load, unload goods or passengers. 7. Where there are yellow lines (during times shown on plates). 8. In a controlled parking zone (during times on plates). 9. Where there are yellow kerb marks (one, two or three). 10. In a 'disc zone' (except with the relevant parking disc). 11. In reserved parking places (for residents or disabled badge holders. 12. At or near a bus stop. 13. At the central reservation of motorways and dual-carriageways. 14. On the zig-zag area of a zebra crossing (except to allow pedestrians to cross). 15. After the rows of studs on approach to a Pelican crossing (except to allow pedestrians to cross). 16. At school entrances or school crossing patrol (at or near). 17. On footpaths or pavements. 18. On or near level crossings (except at red light to wait for a train). 19. Near a junction (within 15m of it). 20. On a bend. 21. At or near the brow of a hill. 22. At or near a hump bridge. 23. Opposite another stationary vehicle (where the road then becomes too narrow). 24. Opposite a traffic island. 25. Alongside another stationary vehicle (double parking). 26. Near road works. 27. On a narrow road. 28. On flyovers or bridges. 29. Inside tunnels or underpasses. 30. On fast main roads (except in a lay-by). 31. On single track roads (and also in any passing place). 32. Where I would block vehicle entrances to properties (driveways, etc). 33. Where I would block the entrance or exit from a car park. 34. Near hospital and ambulance entrances. 35. Near doctors entrances. 36. Near police and fire station entrances. 37. Near a fire hydrant. 38. Near coast guard or life boat station entrances. 39. On right hand side of a road at night (except in one way streets). 40. Near traffic lights. 41. Where I prevent the use of properly parked vehicles.   *Rules 137-141 inc.*

FACT: *Yellow lines along the edge of carriageways indicate that restrictions to parking are in force. Generally, the more paint, the greater the restriction.*

 What should you remember about parking when selecting a position?

A. I need to ask myself, 'Is my car safe, is it parked legally and will I cause any inconvenience to others?' Walking a few extra metres is better than causing an accident.

Rules 138-141 inc.

 What must you do before leaving your vehicle anywhere?

A. I should make sure that the handbrake is on firmly, the engine and headlamps are switched off and the vehicle is locked.   *Rule 137*

Q How close to the kerb should you park?

A. I should stop and park as close as I can to the kerb, without mounting it (endangering pedestrians) or rubbing against it (damaging the tyre walls).   *Rule 137*

Q What should you not use as an excuse for bad or illegal parking? 1. Hazard warning lights. 2. Red triangle. 3. Sidelights.

A. 1.   *Rule 134*

Q These small yellow and blue plates are found near areas of yellow lines and give precise details of the restriction in a given area. Can you explain their meaning?

1   2   3

A. 1. This means there is a continuous no waiting restriction in force. 2. This means there is a parking restriction during the week and covering most of the day. 3. These are found where there are broken yellow lines and refer to limited parking periods.

Q What do these signs mean?

P **Permit holders only**

P **Disabled badge holders only**

A. They show that parking is restricted to either permit holders (possibly residents or professionals) or disabled drivers. Both types of permit should be displayed on the windscreen.

Q What do these two signs mean
and how do they differ?

1   2

A. 1. Waiting restrictions apply — the road edge will give
details either by yellow lines or plates. 2. Clearway — no
stopping on the main carriageway (except at a lay-by) at
any time.

Q Explain this sign.

A. It is an urban clearway sign and means no stopping.
However, the small sign means waiting restrictions are for
set periods. In this instance there is no stopping during
week days, during the early morning and evening. I may
stop for as long as necessary to set down or pick up
passengers.

Q What do yellow bands on the edge of pavements mean?
1. No parking on the pavement. 2. Loading and unloading
restrictions apply. 3. No overtaking.

A. 2.

Q What is the significance of these three yellow stripes
painted on the kerb?

A. They mean that loading and unloading is prohibited during every working day and at other additional times. For example, a confirmation plate may read:

> ## No loading
> ## at any time

Q What is the significance of these two yellow stripes painted on the kerb?

A. They mean that loading and unloading is prohibited during every working day. For example, a confirmation plate may read:

> No loading
> Mon-Sat
> 8·30 am - 6·30 pm

Q What is the significance of a single yellow stripe painted on the kerb?

A. It means that loading and unloading is only restricted during peak periods such as rush hours. For example, a confirmation plate may read:

> No loading
> Mon-Fri
> 8·00 - 9·30 am
> 4·30 - 6·30 pm

Q It is an offence to park your vehicle on common land more than a specified distance from a highway. How far? 1. 10ft. 2. 10m. 3. 15m. 4. 50m.

A. 3.

The Law Demands

Q For how long does setting down and picking up passengers mean? 1. Two minutes. 2. Five minutes. 3. Ten minutes.

A. 1.

Q The Highway Code says you are not allowed to park opposite or nearly opposite another parked vehicle if you will make the road too narrow. However, when is it legal to park this way? 1. When I am stopping to make a telephone call. 2. When the road is wide. 3. When the road is very narrow any way.

A. 2.

Q If you park on one side of the road with another car immediately opposite, how many car widths must you be sure to leave? 1. One car width. 2. Two car widths. 3. Three car widths.

A. 2.

Q What do these two signs indicate?

A. They indicate the beginning and end of a controlled parking zone. The time plate indicates the times and days of restriction.

Q What sort of parking could these signs be an indication of? 1. A meter zone. 2. A free-for-all. 3. A disc zone.

A. 1 and 3.

Q What are the criteria for using meter zones and disc zones?

A. I must park at a meter and pay the required charge before leaving my vehicle. Before parking in a disc zone, I must first apply for a disc and then display it in my windscreen. It is illegal to park in the disc zone without the necessary disc.   *Rules 139 & 141*

Q If you temporarily park your car on yellow lines to load or unload, or to allow passengers to board or alight, how should you let passing traffic know you are stopped? 1. Press on the brake pedal. 2. Put your hazard lights on. 3. Leave a left turn signal on.

Q What does this sign mean, with and without the lower plate?

A. It is a parking place sign, the lower plate indicates there are places for towed caravans.

Night Parking

Q During the night you must park on the right, except when in a one way street, when you must park on the left. True or false?

A. False. During the night I must always park on the left (with the flow of traffic) except in a one way street, when I may park on the right.   *Rules 142 & 143*

Q When parked at night must you leave your sidelights on? 1. Yes. 2. No. 3. Yes, in certain circumstances.

A. 3. It is illegal to park at night without light, unless I am in a road with a maximum speed limit of 30mph, driving a vehicle which does not exceed 1525kg unladen, and at least 10m from a junction and facing in the direction of the traffic or in a recognised parking place.   *Rule 143*

Q Under what circumstances must you always leave your lights on no matter where on the road you are parked at night?

A. I must always leave my lights on if there is fog or if my trailer or vehicle has a projecting load.   *Rules 143 & 144*

Q Where is it best to park if you possibly can? 1. On the road. 2. On a roundabout. 3. Somewhere else.

A. 3. Where possible, I should always pull off the road to a parking area. This could be a car park, forecourt, or a side road, rather than the main road. If I have finished with the vehicle for the day, my driveway, or for maximum security, a garage is much better. *Rule 137*

Q How far from a junction should you park your car? 1. As far as possible. 2. Not within 10m. 3. Not within 15ft.

A. 2. *Rule 140*

Parking on a Hill

Q When parking your car facing uphill, which way should you turn your wheels if there is a kerb on your left? 1. To the right. 2. Keep them straight. 3. To the left.

A. 3.

Q When parked and facing downhill, which way should you turn your wheels? 1. When there is a kerb on the left. 2. When there is no kerb. (a) Keep them straight to facilitate driving away. (b) To the left. (c) To the right.

A. Both 1 and 2 have the same answer, (b).

Q Why do you take these precautions and what else should you remember to do?

A. I want my wheels to be checked by the kerb if the vehicle rolls away in my absence. I should, in addition, remember to apply the handbrake firmly. After the vehicle is switched off I can also select first gear when facing uphill, and reverse gear when facing downhill. In addition, I must remember to select neutral before starting.

Q If you park your car and leave it for a short while with the engine running, are you breaking the law? 1. Only if you leave it for more than two minutes. 2. Yes if you leave it at all. 3. Yes if you are not loading or unloading. 4. No.

Q After parking on the left, what should you be especially careful to look out for before opening the door?

A. If I am getting out of the driver's seat I must first look around and make sure there is no one on the road, either cars, cyclists or motor cyclists, close enough to be hit by my door. If I am getting out on the passenger's side I must first look out for pedestrians, prams and trolleys on the pavement, and be careful not to hit anybody.   *Rule 137*

Q How should you supervise children wishing to get out of the car?

A. I should think of their safety first and let them get out on the pavement side. If they are young, I would first get out before letting them out onto the pavement, so that I can keep them together and in my care.   *Rule 137*

39
Vehicle Security

Q Before leaving your vehicle, what sensible precautions can you take to make sure it's still there when you get back?

A. 1. Remove the ignition key always, even if I am only going to be a minute. 2. Turn the wheel to engage the steering lock. 3. Lock any valuables in the boot or take them with me. 4. Close all the windows tight. 5. Lock all the doors. 6. Take vehicle documents with me. 7. Park in a well lit place.

Q What sort of products could you use for additional security?

A. A locking brace made of really strong metal which hooks onto the steering wheel and clutch pedal or gear lever and handbrake. An alarm which immobilises the ignition or detects vibration and forced entry. A thief would look quite stupid if the object of his activity started wailing at him. The registration number can be etched on all the windows quite cheaply, but are expensive for a thief to replace. *The Highway Code page 75*

40

Breakdowns

Q If your vehicle breaks down on the road, what should you do with it?

A. I should get the vehicle off the road as soon as possible and keep myself, passengers and any animals away from the road edge. *Rule 149*

Q If this isn't possible, for example, when a mechanical problem stops the drive wheels turning, what else can you do? 1. Use your hazard warning lights. 2. 'Bump' the car over sideways. 3. Leave the bonnet open.

A. 1. My hazard warning lights are a visible indication that I have a problem (and that I don't just park like this normally). *Rule 150*

Q What danger are you and your passengers in if you remain in the vehicle?

A. We are in danger of collision by other vehicles.

FACT: *If you have to leave your vehicle to summon help from a garage or the like, organise any passengers first. Make sure they all stay together in a safe place and are aware of the danger they are in. If you break down at night, carry something light or white, when walking to a phone or garage.*

Q If you carry a red warning triangle in your boot, on which side of the road should you place it? 1. On the left. 2. On the right. 3. On the same side of the road as the vehicle. 4. In the middle of the road.

    A. 1 and 3.   *Rule 150*

EXAMPLE: *Suppose you have a tyre blow out and the car finally comes to rest on the right side of the road, facing oncoming cars. Walk down the road toward oncoming traffic and place the triangle on their* left, *because this is the side of the road affected.*   *Rule 150*

Q How far away from the obstruction should you place your warning triangle for the following types of road?
1. A major A road.   (a) 10m.
2. A B road.   (b) 150m.
3. A dual-carriageway.   (c) 50m.
4. A motorway.   (d) 75m.

    A. 1 = (c).   2 = (c).   3 = (b).   4 = (b).   *Rule 150*

Q If you carry traffic cones, how should they be placed to warn of obstruction?

    A. I place the first cone 15m away, on the same side of the road and next to the kerb. The last cone is placed level with the outside of the obstruction, and any extra cones in a line between these two.

Q You break down at night and stand at the rear of the car with your passengers discussing the problem, or you get four burly by-standers to give you a push. What have you done wrong in both instances?

A. I have allowed my rear lights to be obscured and other traffic may not see my car. Two or three people is plenty if the car is to be moved and I should warn them of the danger of covering the lights from other motorists.

Rule 150

Q What do you do if anything falls from your vehicle? 1. Phone the police for assistance. 2. Stop somewhere safe and retrieve it carefully. 3. Stand in front of the object to prevent anyone running over it.

A. 2. Rule 151. (This rule does not apply to motorways: Rule 178.)

NOTE: *Anything which falls from your vehicle, either from the roof rack or part of the vehicle itself (i.e. bumper or exhaust) suggests that you didn't check that it was tied down or secured properly in the first place. As the driver, it is your responsibility to ensure that any load will cause no danger or nuisance to others by falling, overhanging or shifting.*

Rule 29 and The Road User & the Law A) 2) Your Vehicle

Q Every car has problems which are inconvenient and costly. What sensible precautions can you take to ensure your time off the road is kept to a minimum?

A. 1. Carry a properly inflated spare tyre. 2. Carry a spare fan belt. 3. Adhere to the servicing frequency for your car. 4. Carry the proper jack and wheel spanner. 5. Keep a reasonable tool kit available (spanners and screwdrivers). 6. Carry spare bulbs and fuses. 7. Join one of the roadside recovery agencies and always carry membership card and special phone box key.

41

Accidents

Q What indications may lead you to suspect an accident has happened ahead and what should you do about it?

A. I may see warning signs, such as red triangles and the flashing lights of emergency vehicles or traffic ahead may be crawling along or stopped. I would slow down and be prepared to stop in a safe position. Once I have stopped, I can use my hazard lights and also warn other traffic.

Rule 152

NOTE: *Advice about what to do at the scene of an accident can be found in the next section on First Aid.*

 If you are involved in an accident which causes injury or damage to someone else, their property or their animals, what does the law require that you do about it? First, if you are to blame. Second, if the other driver was the cause. Third, when neither of you is at fault.

A. In all cases, whoever is to blame: 1. I must stop. 2. I must give my name, address and the car's registration number to the other driver. Also include the name of my insurance company. 3. Ask the other driver for the same details. 4. If this isn't practicable (for example, the driver of the other vehicle is injured, or if I hit a stationary unoccupied vehicle), report the accident to the police within 24 hours. 5. If any one is injured I must report to the police station within 24 hours and produce my certificate of insurance, either at the time or within seven days.

The Road User & the Law A) 10) Accidents

FACT: *The animals covered by this law include any horse, cattle, ass, mule, sheep, pig, goat or dog.*

 What is the difference between a toughened windscreen and a laminated windscreen, when they are broken in an accident?

A. Toughened windscreens shatter into small rounded pieces and will likely fall out, either into the car or onto the road. They are designed not to cut but vision is seriously impaired. Laminated windscreens are made of two layers of glass with a plastic film sandwiched between them. They crack, but normally stay in place, unless the whole window falls out. Visibility remains good even if the window stays in place.

Toughened glass   *Laminated glass*

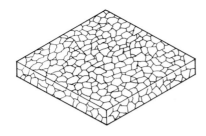

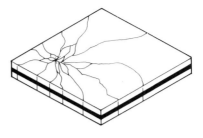

 Q If you are involved in an accident and the other driver refuses absolutely to give their name and address, what do you do? 1. Report the incident to the police. 2. Take the engine number. 3. Shout and scream.

A. 1.

NOTE: *Make a note of the make and model of the car and its registration number. Be extremely suspicious and write down a full description of the driver and any passengers, then give this to the police when you report the accident.*

The Road User & the Law A) 10) Accidents

Accidents Involving Heavy Goods Vehicles

Q Where an accident involves a vehicle containing dangerous goods, what additional information should you gather before requesting assistance from the emergency services?

A. If it is safe, I should look for the hazard information panel on the back of the lorry (it is diamond shaped except for an orange oblong indicating dangerous goods in packages). If there are liquids, powders or gases escaping and I can't see clearly from a distance, I should try to make out the colour(s) of the diamond symbol. I then give this information to the police or ambulance service, who will call the fire brigade so that foaming or washing down can take place as well as victim recovery.   *Rule 154*

Q Once someone has been sent to summon the emergency services, what should you do now?

A. Move away from the vehicle, TOXIC SUBSTANCES CAN KILL. Check the wind direction and select a safe position 'up wind' of the accident. Keep checking in case I should suddenly become surrounded by dust or vapour. Staying too close may cause me serious injury and any attempts to save others should be undertaken with the utmost caution.

Rule 154

FACT: *Exactly what these diamond hazard information panels mean is explained in the section on heavy goods vehicles. Learn these symbols so that you know what sort of cargo the vehicle you are following is carrying. In an accident, though uninjured, you may be exposed to lung damage, skin eruption, allergic reaction, eye damage, sickness from ingested mist and fire. Go to hospital and get yourself checked over, especially if you had anything to do with the rescue operation around the crash site.*

42

*F*irst Aid on the Road

If you come across, or are involved in, a road accident, the Highway Code gives some general advice about what to do, so that the situation doesn't escalate any further. Firstly, act quickly and try not to panic. Every second injured persons go untreated increases the risk to their lives.

 How can you prepare for this if you are suddenly called upon to deal with what will undoubtedly be an unfamiliar situation?

A. Prepare myself now by investing in a first aid handbook and read it so that I am familiar with its contents.

NOTE: *These books are fairly cheap to buy and contain much of the information you will need to cope with injuries at the scene of an accident — informtion that you can teach yourself. Remember, it isn't only others that will be grateful for your help, but members of your own family may depend on your knowledge.*

First aid handbooks contain advice on such subjects as: abdominal injuries, artificial respiration, asphyxiation, back and neck injuries, little and severe bleeding, burns, chest compression, chest injuries, choking, concussion, crush injuries, cuts, fractures, head and facial injuries, heart attack, moving injured people, pulse, shock, splints, sprains and unconsciousness. Note also that artificial respiration and chest compression (for a stopped heart) should be taught to you by a qualified instructor from the St John Ambulance Association, St Andrews Association of the British Red Cross Society.

 What else can you do to make sure you are prepared?

A. Carry a first aid kit in the car.

NOTE: *First aid kits are available from most chemists, already made up, but you usually pay 'over the top' for them. You can make your own using a lined plastic box, and marking it, FIRST AID. The contents should include such things as: soluble painkillers, calamine lotion, antiseptic cream and wipes, waterproof plasters, a roll of 1in (25mm) plaster, gauze, a triangular bandage, open-weave bandage and eye pad, safety pins, round-ended tweezers, round-ended scissors and a small pen torch. Of course all these things should remain unopened and in their packages until needed, to preserve their sterility. I have also found the need to carry a preparation called 'Wasp-eze' during the summer months when over curious children get stung on fishing trips and picnics.*

 What are the two threats that face casualties immediately following a road accident? 1. Fire. 2. Looting. 3. Loss of no claims bonus. 4. Pets running away. 5. Damaged pride. 6. Further collision.

A. 1 and 6.

 If you are first on the scene of an accident, what can you do to prevent further tragedy?

A. 1. Warn other traffic. 2. Switch off the engines of all cars involved and ask any bystanders to do the same to their own vehicles. 3. Ask everyone to extinguish their cigarettes and impose a 'no smoking' ban. *Rule 153*

TIP: *Sniff the air around for petrol fumes from fractured fuel lines. Park your car a little way down the road on the same side as the accident and switch on your hazard warning lights. If you have a red warning triangle or traffic cones, use them. Both these methods are useful if the accident is near a bend.*

 What is the next procedure?

A. I would take charge, if no one else has done so and send someone for an ambulance and the police as soon as possible. Give the emergency services as much information as they ask for.

NOTE: *The exact location is important, so try to establish where you are, on the way to the phone. If you are in an unfamiliar place, note any road signs, street names, large buildings or the town and number in the phone box itself. State the number of casualties and vehicles involved. On the motorway, ask someone to drive on to the next emergency telephone.* Rule 153

 A casualty in the rear passenger seat is crying, but the door is crushed in solid. Should you help them to get out?

A. No, unless the car is in danger of being struck again or of catching fire. If the casualty is crying or moaning they are breathing and I should do my best to console them. Hold a hand, talk and reassure them that an ambulance crew is on the way. *Rule 153*

NOTE: *An inexpertly moved casualty, with an unseen broken neck or spinal injury, may be permanently paralysed. Wait for the medical team. Move uninjured people to a place of safety and out of the risk of fire and collision.* Rule 153

 When would you give a casualty mouth-to-mouth resuscitation?

A. If they were unconscious and breathing had stopped.

NOTE: *A casualty can only live for four to six minutes without air. After that the brain suffers irreversible damage and death soon follows. Until help arrives their lives will depend on you.* The Highway Code page 75

Q Put these instructions for artificial respiration into the correct order.
1. Check again to see if breathing restarts.
2. Clear any obstruction from mouth.
3. Repeat every four seconds until casualty can breath unaided.
4. Check casualty is breathing by 'hearing' for it.
5. If not, pinch casualty's nostrils and blow into mouth gently.
6. Tilt the head backwards as far as possible.
7. Watch for chest to rise, then withdraw.

A. The sequence should read: 4, 2, 6, 1, 5, 7 and 3.

Q If the casualty is unconscious but still breathing, what should the priorities be?

A. I would make sure the victim is not in any more danger, and keep checking that they are still breathing. If breathing becomes very faint or stops altogether I should proceed as for the previous question. I can also lightly cover them with a coat or car rug to prevent them getting cold.

Q How can you help a casualty who is bleeding severely?

A. I can apply firm hand pressure over the wound to staunch the flow of blood (use clean material to cover the wound first if you can find some without wasting time) and keep holding or secure with a pad until the bleeding stops.

NOTE: *Never push on an embedded foreign object and don't try removing it either. Close the skin around it and hold in place with cloth or bandage, on either side, to lessen blood flow. Bleeding can be lessened by raising the limb above the heart, but check first that it is not broken. Start self help treatment for casualties who are bleeding but can hold onto their own* *wounds for a while, and leave yourself free for those with more severe injuries.*

FACT: *Casualties should* never *be given anything to eat or drink until they have been checked over for internal injuries by a trained medical team.*

Q After severe bleeding or trauma, what can you expect a patient to suffer, and what should you do about it?

A. I would expect to see a casualty or frightened person suffer shock. Firstly I would reassure them that they were going to be fine and help was on the way. I'd see that they were comfortable and lightly cover them with a coat or blanket, then, to prevent them moving around, I'd stay close by until help arrived in the form of emergency service personnel. *Rule 153*

43

Motorway Driving

General

 What are motorways?

A. Motorways are dual-carriageway roads with two or three lanes plus an extra lane on the left called a 'hard shoulder'. There are no crossroads, traffic lights, normal junctions, sharp bends, roundabouts or steep hills on motorways. I enter and leave via sliproads on the left.

 Which of the following are excluded from motorways? 1. Pedestrians. 2. Saloon cars. 3. Pedal cyclists. 4. Learner drivers. 5. Heavy goods vehicles. 6. Low powered motorcycles. 7. Certain slow moving vehicles carrying oversized loads (except by special permission). 8. Estate

---

cars. 9. Tractors. 10. Coaches. 11. Combine harvesters. 12. Horse riders. 13. Fire engines. 14. Agricultural vehicles. 15. Invalid carriages under 5cwt. 16. Ambulances. 17. Animals. 18. Vehicles towing trailers. 19. Caravans.

A. 1, 3, 4, 6, 7, 9, 11, 12, 14, 15 and 17.   *Rules 155, 182 & The Road User & the Law* c) Motorway Driving

Q Under what circumstances would you as a learner be allowed to use the motorway?

A. The only circumstance is if I am a heavy goods vehicle learner driver. Otherwise I may only be a passenger.
The Road User & the Law c) Motorway Driving

Q You are about to join a motorway by the slip road and notice a couple of hitch-hikers thumbing a lift. You stop on the left to pick them up. Have you done anything wrong?

A. Yes, in fact we both have. Firstly it is illegal for pedestrians to walk on the motorway or its sliproads and it is illegal for me to stop on any part of a motorway, including its slip roads, except in an emergency.
Rules 6 & 181

Q What two things will you immediately notice about motorway traffic? 1. The faster speed. 2. Two way traffic. 3. One way traffic. 4. Traffic passing on the left. 5. Sharp bends ahead.

A. 1 and 3.   *Rule 156*

Q Because traffic travels faster on motorways, what must you make sure of? 1. About your vehicle. 2. About your driving.

A. 1. I must be able to sum up traffic situations quickly. 2. I need to use my mirrors regularly and look effectively. 3. My continued concentration is doubly important on motorways. 4. My vehicle must be in good mechanical condition and able to cruise at speed. 5. The radiator, oil level and fuel tank should be checked at the start of a journey so that none of them run out and will last, at least, to the next service area. 6. Check that the tyre pressures are correct for motorway driving. 7. Check that all loads, carried or towed, are fully secured.   *Rules 157*

Q What is the motorway speed limit? 1. 60mph. 2. 70mph. 3. 80mph. 4. 100mph.

A. 2. Except for cars towing caravans or trailers and goods vehicles with 7.5 tonnes maximum laden weight for whom the limit is 60mph.

TIP: *When on the motorway and after cruising at speed for a while your own speed will seem much slower than it actually is. This is because of the general openness of motorways where there is nothing near enough to use as a fixed point of reference. On ordinary roads there are permanent buildings and parked cars to use constantly. On the motorway everything is moving, and using other moving traffic as a reference will reduce your interpretation of your own speed, so, check the speedometer regularly.*

Q What makes sliproads and link roads between motorways dangerous?

A. These roads may have sharp bends which I can take safely only if I slow down. Therefore, it is important that I quickly shake off the 'motorway feeling' of speed and make the necessary adjustments.   *Rule 186*

Joining the Motorway

Q From which side of a motorway do you join or leave? 1. On the left. 2. On the right. 3. From a flyover.

A. 1.

Q What type of road do you use to join a motorway and what is its specific purpose?

A. I use a sliproad, an extra lane, which extends for a long distance alongside the existing motorway (called an acceleration lane), before eventually tapering off. Its purpose is for me to accelerate up to the same speed as traffic on my right before joining the motorway.

Q Who must give way to whom when joining a motorway?
1. Motorway traffic gives way to traffic on the sliproad.
2. Motorway traffic must move over to the second lane.
3. Joining traffic gives way to motorway traffic.

A. 3.

Q Describe the procedure you would follow to join a motorway from a sliproad.

A. I am driving down the sliproad and immediately look to acquire some idea of the amount of traffic on the motorway ahead and to the side. Then I indicate right to show that I intend entering the nearside lane (this is particularly important at night as a flashing light attracts more attention than a steady car light). I then look over my shoulder for a suitable, safe gap in the traffic and accelerate along the lane to a matching speed, as I choose my place. If I am waiting for a vehicle to pass I must accelerate to a speed that will allow me to move in behind, and still leave a safe gap. Once into the inside lane I then cancel the indicator and make any final adjustment to my speed so that I don't gain on traffic or baulk any traffic approaching from behind. *Rules 158, 159, 160*

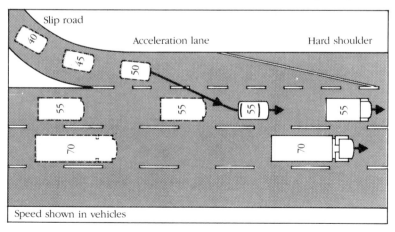

Q Should you overtake the car in front if you are on a sliproad or acceleration lane and have accelerated to a faster speed? 1. Yes. 2. Only if the car in front is towing a caravan. 3. No. Explain your answer.

A. 3. To overtake on a sliproad is very dangerous because the driver in front is concentrating on the traffic already on the motorway. Although the driver probably knows I am behind him, he is likely to be looking for a safe gap and may pull across in front of me. If the driver sees me pulling out, perhaps into the same gap he has chosen, and then notices the acceleration lane is running out, he may brake hard in front of me.

 Once onto the motorway and driving along the inside lane, what should you do next? 1. Overtake as soon as possible to get into the swing of motorway driving. 2. Move to the middle lane. 3. Do not change lanes for two miles. 4. Stay in the left lane long enough to become accustomed to the speed before overtaking. 5. Stay at 60mph for a few minutes.

A. 4.   *Rule 160*

On the Motorway

 There are several manoeuvres which are strictly forbidden on motorways. Can you think what these might be?

A. Reversing, turning in the road, crossing the central reservation and driving against the traffic.   *Rule 163*

 You have joined a motorway from a roundabout and find you are going in the opposite direction to that which you intended. What should you do? 1. Do a U-turn. 2. Reverse back along the hard shoulder and up the sliproad. 3. Carry on to the next exit, leave and rejoin the other carriageway.

A. 3. I must carry on and leave by the next available exit. There may be another roundabout circling above the motorway, or off to one side, so that all I need to do is drive around and re-enter the motorway in the opposite direction.   *Rule 163*

 What speed limits should you not exceed when on the motorway?

A. I must not exceed the national motorway speed limit of 70mph or 60mph for certain vehicles or any indicated speed limit on stretches where there are roadworks or bad weather, nor should I exceed the speed limit for the vehicle I am driving. *Rule 161*

 What should cause you to reduce your speed as a matter of routine?

A. In rain, ice, snow or fog I must KEEP MY SPEED DOWN. *Rules 57 & 58*

TIP: *Whenever you hear of a 'pile up' on the motorway, it is almost always because drivers are travelling too fast in adverse conditions, usually ice, rain, high winds and fog. The rule 'Never drive so fast that you cannot stop well within the distance you can see to be clear' is never more important, but unfortunately never so often ignored, than it is on a motorway.* *Rules 57 & 161*

 What sort of accidents are more common on motorways and why? 1. Head-on collisions. 2. Sideways collisions. 3. Rear-end collisions.

A. 3 is the answer because all traffic is travelling in the same direction.

FACT: *For the most part, drivers on motorways do not allow enough room between themselves and the vehicle in front.*

 What minimum distance should you keep from the vehicle in front for each mph of your speed, assuming dry conditions and that your vehicle is well maintained? 1. One metre or two seconds. 2. Two metres or two seconds. 3. Two metres or three seconds.

A. 1.

TIP: *The following should be regarded as minimum distances. If you don't normally leave this much room, NOW would be a good time to start, before you have an accident. If you regularly drive with a bigger gap I suggest you stick to it.*
In the dry — one metre for each mph or a two second gap.
In the wet — two metres for each mph or a four second gap.
In the ice — ten metres for each mph or a twenty second gap.

Q On the motorway you may be driving for long distances for a long time and for the most part, in a straight line. This can make you feel sleepy. How can you prevent this and what should you do if you feel tired? 1. By taking pills. 2. By getting plenty of fresh air. 3. By turning up the car heating. 4. By pulling over onto the hard shoulder for coffee. 5. Turn up the radio.

A. 2. Fresh air will help for a short while but I must pull into the next service area or turn off at the next exit and walk around. *Rule 162*

NOTE: *Motorway driving takes its toll on car and driver alike. Feeling drowsy during a long drive not only puts you and passengers, but everybody else, at serious risk. It just takes one driver to fall asleep at the wheel, even for a couple of seconds, to cause a major motorway catastrophe.*

TIP: *It is very important that your car remain visible to other drivers for a longer distance than on ordinary roads because of the higher speeds. If there is any doubt about the weather or time of day, switch on your headlights early, don't wait for everyone else. Be a prompter not a copier.*

Lane Discipline

 Q When driving along a two lane motorway, where should you position your vehicle? 1. In whichever lane is most convenient. 2. In the left lane, except when overtaking. 3. In the right lane when turning right.

A. 2. *Rule 164*

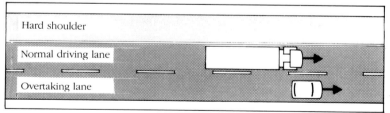

 Q Which overall rule governs your use of a three lane motorway?

A. 'Keep to the left'. *Rule 164*

Q Which is the 'slow lane', the 'mid-speed lane' and the 'fast lane'? 1. The left, middle and right lanes respectively. 2. All lanes are fast lanes. 3. There are no such lanes.

A. 3.

Q What are the rules for using the left lane, the middle lane and the right lane of a three lane motorway?

A. 1. The left lane is for normal driving and I should stay in this lane whenever the road is clear ahead. 2. I may use the middle lane to overtake slower vehicles in the left lane. If there is a long line of slow vehicles I can use this lane until I have passed them. 3. The right lane is for overtaking only, and I would use it when I wish to overtake a slower vehicle occupying the middle lane. *Rule 164*

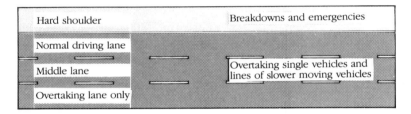

Hard shoulder	Breakdowns and emergencies
Normal driving lane	
Middle lane	Overtaking single vehicles and lines of slower moving vehicles
Overtaking lane only	

Q What must you do once you have overtaken any vehicle(s) in either overtaking lane, and what precautions would you take first?

A. I first make sure that I can see the vehicle(s) I have overtaken in my interior mirror so that I don't cut back in front of them. Then I move back to the left lane, or to the middle lane and then the left lane as soon as I can.
Rules 167, 168 & 169

Q Whereabouts in your lane should you position your car for motorway driving? 1. Over to the left of the lane. 2. In the middle of the lane. 3. To the right of the lane.

A. 2.

Q To help drivers on motorways, there are various coloured studs (cat's eyes) used to show the edges of

the carriageway. Can you match them up?
1. Green studs.
2. Amber studs.
3. Red studs.
(a) Mark the right hand edge of the carriageway.
(b) Mark the left hand edge of the carriageway.
(c) Separate the acceleration and deceleration lanes from the carriageway.

A. 1 — (c). 2 — (a). 3 — (b).   *Rule 174*

Q Where would you see this sign and what does it mean? What must you be prepared for?

A. I may see this sign on relatively steep upward gradients. It indicates an extra crawler lane for heavy, slow moving vehicles, so that they don't impede the flow of faster traffic. I must be prepared to let them come back into the normal left lane at the top and not make the driver stop, as it is very hard for large vehicles to get going again on a hill.

Rule 88

Q On some motorways signs are placed above the road on gantries. These two have different meanings. Do you know what they are telling you?

A. Sign 1 is telling me that the next junction is number 4 and if I want to go to Marlow I should select the lane beneath the arrow. If Oxford is my destination, I should select the middle lane, or, if I am overtaking at the time, go back to the middle lane. After the next junction there are only two lanes of motorway going straight on, so I should get in lane early. Sign 2 is telling me that junction 2 is half a mile away and will take me to Coventry (E) and Leicester if I want to leave the motorway. I may keep to my left lane because the upright arrow tells me that after the sign and junction there remains three lanes of motorway going north west. *Rule 175*

 Driving along a three lane motorway, you are towing a caravan and want to overtake, but the middle lane is full of traffic. Would you: 1. Never overtake, and always drive in the left lane? 2. Use the right hand overtaking lane? 3. Wait for the traffic in the middle lane to move on? 4. Overtake on the left?

A. 3.

 Which of the following types of traffic are banned from the right hand lane of a three lane motorway? 1. Large lorries with an operating weight of over 6 tonnes. 2. Motorcycles. 3. Large lorries with an operating weight of over 7.5 tonnes. 4. Any vehicle drawing a trailer. 5. Cars towing a caravan. 6. A coach over 8m. 7. A bus longer than 12m.

A. 3, 4, 5 and 7. *Rule 166*

NOTE: *When there are exceptional circumstances, such as, signs for roadworks, closed lanes, accidents or police directions, these vehicles may use the outer lane, so watch out for them when selecting your own lane and negotiating any of these hazards.*

Overtaking

 When overtaking on a motorway the procedure is the same as for ordinary roads, but special attention should be paid to one point in particular. Re-cap your overtaking procedure and think of the point in question.

A. I should overtake only on the right (Rule 170) and use my mirrors to make sure the lane I am moving into is clear far enough behind and ahead. Then I must signal before I move out, pass the vehicle(s) in front as quickly as possible and safely, then check my mirrors and signal to move back into my original lane. If I've used the right hand lane I should move to the left lane as soon as the road ahead is clear, or if traffic ahead is a long way off. The special point about motorways is that traffic can be travelling at 70mph in any lane and so a vehicle behind me or in the next outer lane may be approaching much more quickly than I think.

Rules 168 & 169

TIP: *Speed becomes quite deceptive when you're on the motorway for a while. You can quite easily overtake when your speed differential is only two or three miles per hour because of the 'never ending' feeling of a motorway. It doesn't really make much difference if overtaking takes a bit longer, but it does make a difference if your perception of the time taken is equal to that of ordinary roads. On ordinary roads overtaking along half a mile of road is unthinkable, and so you do it quicker. Always make sure you are well clear before pulling back in.*

Rule 169

Q What are the rules about overtaking on the left in motorway traffic?

A. I must never overtake on the left unless traffic is moving slowly in queues and my queue just happens to be moving quicker than the outer lanes. I must never change to a left lane to overtake, either in free traffic or in queued traffic, and never overtake by using the hard shoulder. *Rule 167*

Q When joining a motorway you may overtake on the left in the acceleration lane before entering the left lane. True or false?

A. False. I do not overtake on the left and I must give way to traffic already on the motorway by entering the lane at the same speed as other traffic, in a suitable gap. If this speed is less than my intended entry speed I should slow down and become part of the traffic flow before accelerating.

Q How can you warn the driver ahead that you intend to overtake, when you think he hasn't seen you or when in adverse conditions? 1. Flash your headlights. 2. Sound your horn first. 3. Sound your horn when alongside. 4. Don't bother the driver with your problems.

A. I could flash my headlights (1) not as a declaration of intent, but to warn of my presence and draw the driver's attention to my signal.

TIP: *Indicator signals rarely self-cancel on motorways because you don't turn the wheel enough to operate them when changing lanes. So check and cancel them where necessary after each lane change.*

SUMMARY: *Overtaking on the motorway Rules 164, 168 & 169*

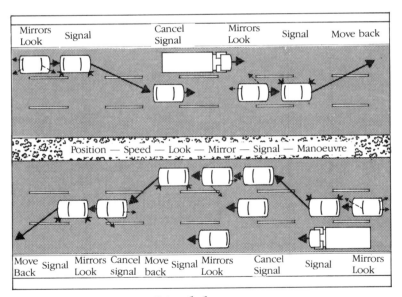

Mirrors Look	Signal		Cancel Signal	Mirrors Look	Signal	Move back

Position — Speed — Look — Mirror — Signal — Manoeuvre

| Move Back | Signal | Mirrors Look | Cancel signal | Move back | Signal | Mirrors Look | | Cancel Signal | Signal | Mirrors Look |

Breakdowns

Q What causes most vehicle breakdowns on motorways?

A. The driver who flogs his car beyond its limits or hasn't taken the trouble to make sure that everything is topped up and in good condition.

Q What instruments have most cars got that can warn of an imminent breakdown and what should you do about them on the motorway?

A. I have got an oil warning light, a battery warning light, a fuel gauge and a coolant temperature gauge. I should keep an eye on them so that I can monitor the mechanical condition of my car.

Q What should you do if you have a mechanical problem with your vehicle on the motorway? 1. Get the vehicle off the carriageway and onto the hard shoulder. 2. Slow down but keep going. 3. Stop at the next service area.

A. 1.

NOTE: *Getting off the motorway is rarely a problem because even if the engine cuts out, a car will still roll forward by its own momentum long enough for you to steer onto the hard shoulder.*

Q If you didn't spot an emergency telephone when you pulled over, how far is the nearest telephone and how will you know which is closest?

A marker post sign showing the way to the nearest telephone.

Emergency telephone boxes like this are connected directly with the police.

A. Emergency telephones are spaced at about one mile intervals, so the furthest you will be away from one, either ahead of you or back along the hard shoulder, will be half a mile. Marker posts along the back of the hard shoulder, at 110 yard intervals, have an arrow pointing to the nearest telephone. *Rule 183*

 Where on the hard shoulder should you position your vehicle? 1. Into the middle of the lane. 2. As far left as possible. 3. Just left of the carriageway.

A. 2. *Rule 183*

 When you are safely on the hard shoulder following a breakdown, what points can you think of which will affect your safety from now until the police arrive?

A. 1. Never forget the danger from passing traffic.
2. Switch on my hazard warning lights.
3. At night, leave my sidelights on.
4. Get out of the car on the embankment side.
5. Never open the doors nearest the carriageway.
6. Adults must get out first to supervise any children.
7. Never stand at the rear of the vehicle.
8. Never stand on the carriageway side of the car.
9. Get off the hard shoulder and wait on the embankment, if possible.
10. Walk to the nearest emergency telephone, keeping well away from the carriageway.
11. Never cross the motorway to use an emergency telephone.
12. Don't leave the vehicle unattended for very long.
13. Never let children or animals wander about on the hard shoulder.
14. Keep animals in the vehicle. *Rule 183*

 If you have a red warning triangle, how far down the carriageway from your vehicle should you place it, and where? 1. On top of the phone box. 2. On the hard shoulder. 3. In the left lane. (a) 150m. (b) 250m. (c) 50m.

A. 2 and (a). *Rule 150*

200

If your breakdown was caused by a minor fault, such as a flat tyre, and you have fixed it again, what is the procedure for rejoining the motorway? 1. Look for a safe gap then start off into the left lane. 2. Drive along the hard shoulder to the next exit and rejoin again properly. 3. Drive along the hard shoulder to a 'matching speed' and move into a safe gap.

A. 3.   *Rules 183 & 184*

NOTE: *The police will tell you how to rejoin the carriageway before you move off, and will then wait until you have done so safely before they themselves leave.*

Obstructions

You are going on holiday and have your luggage stowed on the roof rack. Suddenly a suitcase falls onto the motorway into the path of other traffic. What should you do? 1. An emergency stop. 2. Forget it and carry on. 3. Stop at the next emergency telephone and inform the police. 4. Pull onto the hard shoulder and retrieve it carefully. 5. Flag down the next passing police car.

A. 3. I may stop on the hard shoulder as this constitutes an emergency and ring the police, who will come to remove the obstruction. I should never attempt to retrieve the article myself as this is highly dangerous.

TIP: *When tying down articles onto your car use plenty of rope, or straps, not the least possible. The forces of lift under a roof rack are tremendous, and increase with speed. On a motorway you also have to account for increased wind, both head on and from the side.*

 On the motorway you notice a ladder half-on/half-off the right hand lane and assume it has fallen from another vehicle. What should you do? 1. Stop on the hard shoulder at the next telephone and inform the police. 2. Leave it because somebody else has obviously done so already.

A. 1. The fact that it is still there suggests that the police don't already know about it. Even if they do, they won't mind your telling them again.

Motorway Signals

 Q What is the main feature of motorway signals?

A. They are normally blank and only come on when the conditions ahead pose a threat to drivers. For example, I may be heading into thick fog, an accident which involves lane closures or icy conditions and the risk of skidding.

Q What happens when the signals are operating? 1. Green lights flash around a yellow panel. 2. Flood lights shine on the road. 3. Amber lights flash around a central panel.

A. 3.   *Rule 171*

Q What is the general message of flashing amber lights?

A. There is danger ahead.

 Q Where will you find these motorway signals and how far apart are they?

A. Sometimes behind the hard shoulder, but mostly along the central reservation, at intervals of not more than two miles. They apply to all lanes facing the sign. On some very busy motorways the signals are on gantries so that there is one signal for each lane and any signal applies only to that lane.   *Rule 170*

Q You see a signal restricting your speed or closing your lane, but cannot see the reason for it. What should you do about it? 1. Ignore it. 2. Obey it anyway. 3. Assume it is a mistake but drive carefully.

A. 2. It is essential for the police to warn traffic in advance, so that lane control changes and speed restrictions can take effect *before* the danger. The motorway signals are there for my safety and I must always act on them.

Rules 171 & 173

Q What does this signal mean: 1. When on the roadside? 2. When on an overhead gantry?

A. The amber lights are warning lights and the '50' legend is the temporary maximum speed limit. The roadside sign covers all lanes, the overhead signal covers the lane below the signal. Other speed limits, 20, 30 or 40 may otherwise be shown.   *Rule 171*

Q What does this signal mean and what could be the cause?

A. Again, flashing amber lights are a warning. The legend means that the right hand lane is closed ahead.

NOTE: *Other configurations will show which lane is closed.*

Rules 171 & 172

Q   What does this sign mean?

A. The danger has passed and the restriction is ended. The lanes are now open and any temporary speed limit is cancelled. I notice that the legend is showing, but the amber lights are off.   *Rule 171*

Q   Signs like these are found on overhead gantries, so do you know what they mean?

A. 1. Change to the next left lane. 2. Leave the motorway at the next exit. 3. Do not proceed any further in this lane.
                                      Rules 171 & 172

Q   A set of signals like this may appear on busy motorways when there is a hazard ahead. Can you explain?

A. The left and middle lanes are restricted to a maximum speed of 50mph and any overtaking vehicles should move to the left by one or two lanes and reduce speed.
                                      Rule 171

Q On approach to a hazard signals may change, giving new instructions, like this. What do they mean?

1   2

3   4

A. 1. Right hand lane closed. 2. End of hazard. 3. Temporary maximum speed of 50 mph. 4. Fog ahead.

Q What do you do if there are flashing red lights above all lanes? 1. Leave at the next exit. 2. Park on the hard shoulder. 3. Slow down and stop at the signals.

A. 3. The road ahead is completely blocked, probably by an accident. When stopped, use your hazard warning lights and if cars are approaching from behind, keep your foot on the brake to show that you have stopped. Switch off your hazard lights before moving away again. *Rule 172*

Q You are about to enter the motorway via a sliproad and notice flashing red lights at the entrance, what do you do? 1. Proceed carefully onto the motorway because there has been an accident. 2. Park on the sliproad. 3. Reduce speed. 4. Do not join the motorway.

A. 4. *Rule 172*

Q An early type of motorway signal has flashing amber lights, one over the other (instead of a double pair of amber lights) at the entrances and at one or two mile intervals. They are gradually being replaced by the modern ones, but until then, what is their message?

A. Danger ahead — (accident, fog, risk of skidding, high winds) slow down to 30mph or less and stay below 30mph until I am sure it is safe to go faster.

Signs

Q What is the chief feature of motorway signs? 1. They have green backgrounds. 2. They have blue backgrounds. 3. They have white backgrounds.

A. 2.   *The Highway Code page 61*

Q What does this sign mean?

A. It is sign indicating the start of the motorway and the point from which motorway traffic regulations apply.

Q Where will you find a sign like this one?

A. At any junction leading directly to a motorway. Its blue colour indicates that the road is a motorway route and the motorway symbol means that motorway regulations apply immediately I turn in that direction.

Q Where will you find a sign like this and what facilities are usually available?

A. It is a service area sign and there will shortly be a sliproad on the left so that I may leave the motorway. The operator's name may be shown at the top. The facilities normally include: petrol, other fuels, refreshments, toilets and telephones. This one also has facilities for the disabled, tourist information and accommodation.

 Where would you see a sign like this?

A. It is a route confirmation sign, and is placed after the exit I have just passed, so that I can assure myself that I am still going in the right direction.

Stopping and Parking

 Some of Britain's motorways pass through beautiful scenery. Hills and cliffs, valleys, woods, ancient buildings and castles all catch the eye of passing travellers. Can you stop to take photographs?

A. No. However much my passengers plead, I must never stop on a motorway for sightseeing, picnics, a rest or for my album.

Q When are you allowed to stop on the motorway? 1. In an emergency. 2. To use a toilet. 3. To prevent an accident. 4. When you need a rest. 5. When you break down. 6. When a police officer signals you to do so. 7. At flashing amber light signals. 8. At flashing red light signals.

A. 1, 3, 5, 6 and 8.   *Rule 179*

Q The only place you are allowed to park on a motorway is in the service area. True or false?

A. True.   *Rule 180*

Q Where must you never park on the motorway?

A. I must never park on the carriageway itself, on the sliproads, on the hard shoulder (except in an emergency) or on the central reservation. *Rule 180*

Q Are you allowed to walk on the carriageway?

A. No never, but I may walk on the edge of the hard shoulder, away from the traffic, to reach an emergency telephone. *Rule 182*

Road Works

Motorways need regular and essential maintenance or improvements. This requires that lanes or complete carriageways are closed, sometimes for weeks or months. Where the carriageway remains closed it will be necessary to move traffic across the central reservation and work a 'contra-flow' system.

FACT: *These are advance warning and 'courtesy' signs for road works.* *Rules 147, 148 & 177*

NOTE: *Maximum speeds are sometimes indicated; you may need to travel slower.*

Q What special care is needed at motorway road works?

A. I must observe signs and signals, reduce my speed, check my mirrors and get into the right lane early while always keeping a safe distance from the vehicle in front.
Rules 147, 148 & 177

FACT: *These signs are used on the carriageway on which the works are taking place.*

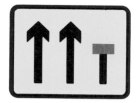  

Their explanation is:
1. *The right lane is closed.*
2. *The two open lanes will shortly be guided over to the opposite carriageway by cones.*
3. *Shortly, the road works will be past and traffic will return to the original carriageway.*

FACT: *If you see this sign it means that either you are being diverted to make way for a contra-flow system with traffic from the opposite carriageway, or just that two of your lanes are closed.*

This sign means that the works or contra-flow system is ending and you will shortly be diverted back to the main carriageway where all three lanes are once again available.

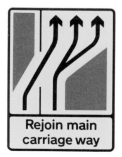

Q Sometimes other arrangements are necessary when the previous systems aren't practical. Can you explain these signs?

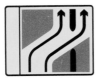 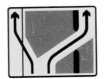 

A. 1. The two left lanes are closed. An extra lane has been made available, but the outer lane crosses the central reservation into contra-flow.

2. All three normal lanes are closed. Two new lanes are made available by using the hard shoulder, and another lane by crossing the central reservation into a contra-flow system.

3. Traffic in contra-flow is about to return to its original carriageway and should be prepared to allow for traffic on the left.

FACT: *A 'courtesy' sign indicates the end of road works.*

Leaving the Motorway

Q The town or city you are going to is off the motorway and to the left. How do you reach it?

A. By taking the preceding slip road on the left.

Q The town or city you are going to is off the motorway and to the right. How do you reach it? 1. By using the sliproad on the right. 2. By using the sliproad on the left. 3. By taking the third exit from the motorway roundabout.

A. 2. Unless I am going to the end of a motorway I always leave on the left. To turn right I can use the roundabout circling above or to the side of the motorway and reach my destination by ordinary roads. *Rules 165 & 185*

Q Describe the sequence you would use to leave the motorway at the next exit.

A. First of all, if I'm not there already, I must move over to the left lane by following the Mirror — Signal —Manoeuvre routine, and where necessary adjust my speed for this lane. I should check all the signs to make sure I have the correct exit. Use my mirrors early and signal left in plenty of time before entering the deceleration lane, looking out for the countdown markers. I must reduce speed gradually before driving up the sliproad.

Q What is the deceleration lane for?

A. It allows me to leave the carriageway at normal motorway speeds so that I don't have to slow down in front of left lane traffic before leaving. It allows me time to slow before entering the sliproad. *Rule 185*

Leaving a motorway

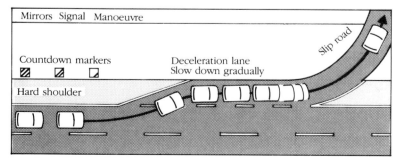

211

TIP: *Never be tempted to change gear in the deceleration lane until you are sure the vehicle will accept it. You may think you are doing 25mph, when in fact you are still at 50mph, or more. Slow down before changing and leave it until you are in the sliproad, at or on approach to the Give Way lines at the end of the sliproad.*

Q How can you best plan a journey that involves travelling on a motorway?

A. Modern maps usually include the junction numbers in little circles, where the motorway is joined from ordinary roads. I can use these numbers to plan in advance my exit and also plot my progress along the motorway.

FACT: *There are normally three main signs at each exit on a motorway.*

Q Where is a sign like this located and what does it tell you?

A. This type of sign occurs one mile before the exit. It just gives the main road number leading off the motorway and also the junction number.

Q Where is a sign like this located and what does it tell you?

A. This type of sign occurs about half a mile before the exit and shows the main traffic destination, road number and junction number.

Q And this sign?

A. It is the last information sign and occurs at the beginning of the deceleration lane. The principal destinations reached by staying on the motorway are also shown.

FACT: *It isn't practical to give drivers vast amounts of information on these signs as you will be zipping past at high speed. This means it is very important that you plan in advance the exit number you require. Once you reach the end of the sliproad (often a roundabout) more information is displayed about your intended destination.*

Q How do you know that you are coming to the deceleration lane?

A. There are countdown markers situated 300, 200 and 100 yards before the exit. They look like this:

Q You have accidentally driven past your exit and this will make you late for an appointment. What can you do? 1. Drive on to the next exit and be late. 2. Drive up the sliproad that leads onto the motorway a little further along. 3. Reverse along the hard shoulder. 4. Turn around in the road and head back.

A. 1. I would never do any of the others. *Rule 163*

Q When leaving the motorway what must you remember to do about the road you are joining?

A. I must remember to adjust my speed to suit the traffic conditions and speed limits on the ordinary roads that I will be using.

TIP: *Continually check your speedometer upon leaving a motorway. The sliproads often have sharp bends so they can easily join ordinary roads at a suitable point. It will take several minutes to readjust to normal road speeds and you can find yourself inadvertently speeding quite easily. However, this is no excuse if you're caught in a speed trap.* *Rule 186*

Q What does this sign mean?

A. End of motorway and its regulations.

44
Motor Cyclists and Moped Riders

Most of the Highway Code rules which apply to motor drivers, such as those relating to pedestrian crossings, alcohol, lines and lanes, roundabouts, signs, speed limits and signals by the police, also apply to you. However, because of your generally greater vulnerability to injury on the roads, there are a few additions to these rules.

Q What items must a motor cyclist, scooter or moped rider have and use, when riding on the road?

A. A safety helmet, of approved design which must be securely fastened. *Rule 30*

Q What other equipment is of extra special importance to riders?

A. Sturdy boots, gloves and reflective (at night) or fluorescent (by day) materials. *Rule 30*

Q What sort of clothing should you wear?

A. I should wear the best quality motorcycle clothes I can afford, on top of my normal clothes.

FACT: *It cannot be overstressed that keeping warm on a motorbike is important. When you are cold, your reaction time is increased, you feel numb and uncomfortable, it becomes more difficult to use foot pedals and handlebar levers.*

Q What part of the road system is forbidden to riders of low-powered machines? 1. Lay-bys. 2. Car parks. 3. Motorways. 4. One way streets.

A. 3.
Rule 155 & The Road User & the Law C)Motorway Driving

Q One part of your machine in particular must comply with the law. Which part? 1. Your ignition system. 2. Your exhaust system and silencer. 3. Your clothing.

A. 2. Remember also your tyres, lights and brakes must also be in good order and efficient.
The Road User & the Law A) To the Drivers of Motor Vehicles

Q Why is it important that motor cyclists observe all of the requirements of the Highway Code and adopt a strict attitude to the correctness of their driving? There are several reasons.

A. 1. I am more vulnerable than motor vehicle drivers because I am not surrounded by a metal cage. 2. I am only about one third as wide as a car and not so easily seen. 3. During a collision I may be thrown clear of the accident itself, but from there, into the path of another vehicle.

Q How can you increase your chances of being seen by others when on a motorcycle?

A. I can use dipped headlights, day and night.

NOTE: *It might cost you a few miles per gallon in economy, but think of your own safety as being more important.*

Q How many passengers can you carry on a two-wheeled machine?

A. One passenger, seated behind the driver.

The Road User & the Law B) To Motorcyclists & Moped Riders

Q What rules apply to carrying a passenger? 1. Passengers must sit astride the cycle. 2. Female passengers may sit 'side saddle' if wearing a dress. 3. There must be a proper seat securely fastened. 4. Passengers can sit on a cushion on the tank if necessary. 5. Passengers can rest their feet on the mud guard or wheel nuts. 6. There must be proper foot rests. 7. Passengers aren't covered by the helmet rules and may wear a coat hood or scarf. 8. Passengers must wear a regulation safety helmet.

A. 1. True. 2. False. 3. True. 4. False. 5. False. 6. True. 7. False. 8. True.   *Rule 30 & The Road User & the Law* B)

Q When wishing to overtake another vehicle or change lanes on your motorcycle, what sequence should you follow?

A. I would first check that the road ahead is clear and then check my mirror. I must then look behind and to my offside before signalling and moving around or over. If I am changing from the right to the left hand lane, I would check over my left shoulder before signalling and moving.

NOTE: *As cycles rarely have as many mirrors as a car, the Mirror – Signal – Manoeuvre routine isn't enough to ensure your safety. Looking behind can help overcome this.*

Rules 51 & 99

Q Some immature motor cyclists have a habit of roaring up *between* queues of traffic, to get to the traffic lights or to the front of a traffic jam. What is the main danger here?

A. 1. Traffic could start moving again and the gap between cars or lorries may be suddenly reduced to almost nothing. 2. A split second of bad judgement can cause a cyclist to hit an overhanging wing mirror or bumper, resulting in the rider being knocked off and perhaps thrown under the wheels of a car or lorry. 3. Pedestrians are sometimes tempted to walk in between queues of stationary traffic to cross the road and may be hidden from view, behind taller vehicles.

45
Heavy Goods Vehicles

Q What makes a vehicle a heavy goods vehicle? 1. Vehicles over 4000kg maximum gross weight. 2. Vehicles over 7500kg maximum gross weight. 3. Trailers over 3500kg maximum gross weight.

A. 2 and 3 are correct. *The Highway Code page 66*

Q Heavy goods vehicles are required to have striped markings fitted on the back. What colour are they? 1. Red and yellow. 2. Red and white. 3. Yellow and white.

A. 1 is correct and they look like this:

The Highway Code page 66

Q What other sign may you see and what are these markings for?

A. I may also see signs like these:

LONG VEHICLE

They are to warn me of the lorry's
presence, and to remind me that
it will take longer to overtake them and for the driver to
overtake me.

Q Lorries which have an overhanging load of more than
2m at the front or rear, such as a crane jib, must carry
projection markers like this:

1   2

Where will you find them positioned?

A. 1 is fitted onto the side of the projection. 2 is fitted onto
the end.   *The Highway Code page 66*

Q What do these signs mean?

A. 1. No vehicles over height shown. 2. No vehicles over
width shown. (Signs may have metric units as well.)

Q How do these signs affect the movement of heavy goods vehicles? What do they mean?

1   2   3   4

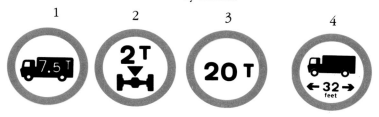

A. They restrict the movement of vehicles over unsuitable ground, roads and bridges. They mean: 1. No goods vehicles over the maximum gross weight shown in tonnes (7.5 tonnes). 2. No vehicles over weight shown in tonnes, including load (total weight limit — 20 tonnes). 3. Axle weight limit in tonnes (2 tonnes). 4. No vehicles or combinations of vehicles over length shown — may also be in metric units (32 ft).

Transport Hazard Information System

 Q The lorry in front of you probably carries a hazard information panel. Can you match the hazard with the colour and symbol of the panel?

Hazard	Colour	Symbol
1. Toxic substance/ toxic gas.	A. Black and white.	I. Black gas cylinder.
2. Compressed gas.	B. Yellow.	II. Sectioned circle with black triangles and a dot.
3. Corrosive substance.	C. White.	III. Black flames.
4. Spontaneously combustible substance.	D. Green.	IV. 'O' with black flames.
5. Oxidizing agent.	E. Red.	V. Skull and crossbones.
6. Radioactive substance.	F. Red and white.	VI. Pouring test tubes onto bar together with hand.
7. Flammable liquid.		

A. 1. C.–V. 2   I. 4. F.–III. 5. B.–IV. 6. C.–II. 7. E.–III.

Q   When are these panels helpful?

A. If the lorry is involved in an accident, I can inform the emergency services of the type of hazard they are likely to encounter on arrival.

TIP: *When you are driving around, make a point of checking the hazard symbol on lorries, so that you know what they are carrying. Give the lorry plenty of room on the road and when manoeuvring.*

46

Heading for Danger

Q   What do these signs mean? What sort of things are covered by the second sign and how are these shown?

A. 1. Means slippery road ahead. 2. Means danger ahead, and can be placed near factory entrances, heavy goods depots, farms, fire stations and near any other danger which does not have a specific sign. A plate below the sign indicates the nature of the danger.

FACT: *There are several potentially dangerous situations which can occur during normal driving which need to be rectified by specific actions on your part. These include skidding, aqua-planing and a tyre blow-out.*

 Q If you were driving along at 55mph and suddenly your front tyre burst, what should you do? 1. Curse, for not having checked them. 2. Hold the steering wheel firmly. 3. Brake hard. 4. Change down to third gear. 5. Let the car roll to a stop.

A. 2 and 5 are correct.

 Q What will happen if you brake hard? 1. The car will swerve right. 2. The car will swerve or weave. 3. The car will tip over.

A. 2. The direction of swerve will depend on which tyre has burst. The car may tip over if I hit anything during the serve.

Q When driving through a flooded area, what points should you remember?

A. 1. Check the depth of water first. 2. Drive slowly — water thrown up inside the engine compartment may drown the ignition system. 3. Slip the clutch to keep the engine speed up but the actual speed down. 4. Try my brakes afterwards to check that they still work properly.

Q You find your brakes don't work after driving through a flood. What is wrong?

A. They are wet and need drying out. If it is safe, I should drive slowly and press lightly on the brake pedal with my left foot. This will cause the pads and shoes to rub against the disc or drum and warm up enough to dry them.

 Q What is aqua-planing? 1. Driving over a flood without sinking into it. 2. Brake failure. 3. Loss of steering and braking. 4. Tyres not in contact with the road.

A. 3 and 4 are correct.

Q Aqua-planing is caused by driving too fast over a thin sheet of water on the road caused by heavy rain. True or false?

A. True.

 Q What will happen to the steering? 1. It feels light. 2. It feels heavy. 3. It feels wobbly.

A. 1.

NOTE: *Steering feels light because the wheels are riding on water and are not in contact with the road.*

Q How can you stop aqua-planing and regain control over the steering and braking? 1. Brake. 2. Come off the accelerator. 3. Push the clutch pedal down.

A. 2.

NOTE: *Engine braking will cause the car to slow down because this has to do with the relationship between engine speed and road wheel speed. Braking will cause the wheels to lock because they are practically free-wheeling over the film of water and pushing down the clutch pedal will cause loss of engine braking, making matters even worse. The best advice, of course, is to slow down in the wet.*

FACT: *Skidding. As a driver it is important to remember that you are responsible for your car skidding — not the car, the road or the weather.*

 Q In what ways can you prevent skids occurring?

A. By driving more slowly in wet, muddy or icy conditions, and spreading my braking out over a greater distance by watching for danger areas, such as sharp bends and side roads and keeping well back from the car in front. Also by keeping my car in a well maintained condition.

Q What could cause your vehicle to skid, should you make a mistake?

A. 1. Harsh and uncontrolled braking. 2. Severe movement of the steering wheel. 3. Sudden or heavy acceleration. 4. Running my car with worn tyres. 5. Cornering too quickly, and 6. Failing to adjust my driving to account for rain, ice, snow, oil or dust.

Q What causes the rear wheels to lock when you brake hard? 1. The weight of the car is thrown forward. 2. The car is thrown sideways. 3. The weight of the car is thrown to the rear.

A. 1.

FACT: *Harsh braking causes the weight of the car to be thrown forward and this adds to the already heavy engine area. Because less weight is over the rear wheels, they lose their grip and lock. Where braking is continued the front wheels may also lock, but, the extra weight will delay this for a moment, giving time for the rear wheels to start to slide sideways.*

Q What should you do if your vehicle starts to skid? 1. Brake harder. 2. Apply the handbrake. 3. Come off the brake. 4. Change gear.

A. 3. I'd first release the brakes then reapply them more gently.

Q What makes a skid more dangerous if braking is harsh? 1. Smoking at the same time. 2. Steering at the same time. 3. Accelerating at the same time.

A. 2.

Q Why is a braking- and steering-related skid more dangerous?

A. Because the weight of the car is thrown over to the outside front wheel of the turn and not just to the overall front of the car.

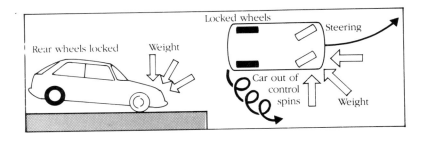

Rear wheels locked · Weight · Locked wheels · Steering · Car out of control spins · Weight

Q What would be the likely outcome of a braking and steering skid if you didn't correct it in time?

A. The car could spin.

Q Why is this dangerous?

A. Apart from the fact that I am out of control, if my car hits anything, such as a kerb, it is likely to flip over onto its roof, and roll.

Q What does 'steer into the skid' mean? 1. Steer the way the car slides. 2. It only applies to a front wheel skid. 3. Use the right hand lane to straighten up.

A. 1.

FACT: *If the rear of the car is sliding left, you should steer left, bringing the front wheels into line with the rear ones. If the rear of the car is sliding right you should steer right. There is a very real danger of overcorrect if you're not careful, which could cause an opposite skid. Always come off the brake and if the skid isn't due to braking, come off the accelerator.*

TIP: *If you are involved in a skid, try to keep your head. By having a thorough understanding of what is happening and knowing how to put it right, you will likely get away with just a scare. If you panic or freeze, with your foot hard down on the brake, the car will take much longer to stop and you will invariably make matters worse, perhaps causing injury to yourself and others.*

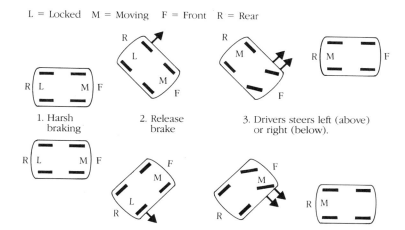

L = Locked   M = Moving   F = Front   R = Rear

1. Harsh braking

2. Release brake

3. Drivers steers left (above) or right (below).

NOTE: *If you happen to be steering (right or left) at the same time at 1, the corrective action remains the same, you will just need more of it.*

Q What do you do if you have a front wheel skid? 1. The same as for a rear wheel skid. 2. Release the accelerator. 3. Nothing.

A. 2. It is important not to steer until the car regains its grip on the road.

47
Mathematics and Forces

The attitude that you as a driver develops, while learning and driving generally, is so important, that lives will depend on it. This applies from the moment you move out from the side of the road on your first lesson, to the time you give up driving.

The qualities which make you a good driver show in the techniques, common sense and courtesy shown in the way you handle yourself and your vehicle.

Responsibility = Concern for your safety and that of others.
Responsibility + Good judgement = A safe margin.
Concentration + Responsibility = Planned and correct action.
Concentration + Momentary distraction = Mistakes and accidents.
Concentration + Anticipation = Experience and safe motoring.
Anticipation + Patience = Accident free driving.
Anticipation + A bad temper = Rash and mindless corrective action.
A bad temper + Over confidence = Carelessness and bad judgement.
A traffic jam + Patience = A safe return to normal driving.
Illness or tiredness = Longer reaction times and late everything.
Experience + Concentration = Confidence
Knowledge of a car's construction + adopting a sympathetic driving technique = Less maintenance + Lower running costs.

Q Two vehicles are approaching each other at 45mph. The gap between them is closing at what speed? 1. 90mph. 2. 45mph. 3. 75mph. 4. 67.5mph.

A. 1.

Q What would be the crash speeds if (a) The cars hit each other, or (b) one of them went into a wall?

A. If the cars hit each other the crash speed would be 90mph. If one hit a wall the crash speed would be 45mph.

Q If you are travelling at 55mph and a car runs into the back of you at 70mph, what is the crash speed? 1. 125mph. 2. -15mph. 3. 15mph. 4. 70mph.

A. 3 is right, because relative to my own speed, the vehicle is only doing 15mph.

Q When judging the distance between yourself and the car in front, it is helpful to be able to convert mph into feet per second. Assuming that mph x 1.5 = ft per second, how many ft per second would you be travelling at the following speeds? 20mph, 30mph, 40mph, 50mph, 60mph, 70mph.

A. 30ft/second, 45ft/second, 60ft/second, 75ft/second, 90ft/second, 105ft/second.

FACT: *The sort of thing that increases your car's fuel consumption is: too much choke to start, rapid acceleration, harsh braking, delayed gear changing, high speeds over short distances, carrying roof racks or carrying unnecessary weight, switching on the lights unnecessarily, worn or incorrectly adjusted ignition and a rich petrol mixture.*

Q When is a moving vehicle most stable? 1. When it is moving forward in a straight line. 2. When being driven at a constant speed. 3. Both of these.

A. 3.

Q Lifting forces increase as: 1. Speed is increased? 2. Light braking is applied? 3. Spoilers are fitted?

A. 1.

Q Downward forces increase as: 1. Speed is increased? 2. Braking is applied? 3. The driver is changing gear?

A. 2.

Q Lifting forces have the effect of reducing steering control. True or false?

A. True.

Q How do these forces affect the movement of your vehicle? Friction, Gravity, Inertia, Momentum, Centrifugal force.

A. Friction — between the road and your tyres is constantly trying to slow the vehicle down. Gravity — holds my vehicle to the ground and is responsible for the weight of the vehicle. Inertia — is a tendency of my vehicle weighted by its passengers to want to stay still until forced to move, giving the feeling of acceleration. Momentum — is the impetus of my vehicle, being the product of its mass and velocity. Centrifugal force — is the outward force felt when on a curved path.

Q How does your car overcome all of these forces and how can you reduce their effects, or compensate for them in your driving?

A. I burn petrol, which produces energy enough to overcome these forces. I reduce their effect by 'reading the road' ahead and acting early on what I see, reducing speed where necessary.

Friction — Control of my car is totally dependant on friction because it keeps the car stable and produces a resistance when in contact with the road. Skidding, ice, dust and wet roads cause a loss of friction.

Gravity — Because of the camber of the road, my vehicle is constantly drawn to the left. I compensate for this with the steering. Heavy vehicles burn more petrol to overcome this force.

Inertia — Is associated with acceleration, braking and cornering. I can reduce the effect of inertia by gentle use of the controls.

Momentum — Means that it takes longer to stop as speed increases. By driving at a reasonable speed for the conditions, I can reduce the amount of braking necessary and the length of time this takes.

Centrifugal force — The outward forces acting on my vehicle and passengers when cornering can be reduced by slowing down before the bend.

Q Applying the brakes on a straight road moves the centre of gravity to the rear and causes the back wheels to grip more. True or false?

A. False. Exactly the opposite is true.

Q Applying your brakes harshly is more likely to cause which wheels to lock and skid? 1. The front wheels. 2. The rear wheels. 3. All the wheels.

A. 2.

Q When does steering become harder? 1. When braking. 2. When accelerating. 3. When negotiating a chicane.

A. 1.

Q When braking and steering on a bend, the weight of your vehicle is thrown onto which wheels? 1. The front wheel on the inside of the curve. 2. The front wheels equally. 3. The front wheel on the outside of the curve.

A. 3.

FACT: *The best way to keep your car under control on a bend is to do all your braking before the bend, select the correct gear and enter the bend under gentle power.*

48
Tips for Manoeuvring

Moving Off

Uphill (Hillstarts) and at an Angle

Moving Off from the side of the road on level ground is one of the first things you will learn when starting to drive. Moving away from the kerb at an angle, for example, from behind a parked car, or on a gradient, entails refining this technique slightly.

The reason for learning this important skill is simply that, when you are stationary, queued up in traffic on a hill, you've got to be able to move off without rolling into the car behind you. If you live on a hill, neighbourly relations would surely suffer greatly if you continually shunted other people's cars up or down a few feet before pulling away.

Your examiner will expect to see that you have full control over your car when pulling out from behind another one or starting off up a hill. Very often both of these exercises are performed together. Practise them separately first and then combine the two when you have mastered both. When you have stopped on the gradient, your examiner expects you to realise you are on a hill and to perform a 'hillstart'.

1. When instructed, find somewhere convenient to pull up on the left, incorporating, if required, the additional instruction to stop about two car lengths behind the parked car in front of you.

NOTE: *There are only two things that are slightly different as far as control of the car is concerned. The steeper the hill, the faster the engine speed you will need, and, the time you release the handbrake is slightly changed.*

2. A skill that you will perfect here is balancing the car on the clutch at the clutch position called the 'biting point'.

3. Press the clutch down with your left foot and select first gear.

4. Press the accelerator with your right foot so that the engine is running faster than it would be for moving off on level ground. Keep your foot steady.

5. Let the clutch up gently and smoothly until you hear the note of the engine drop slightly. You have found the 'biting point'. The car may also try to move forward very slightly but not with any force.

6. Hold your feet perfectly still. Only now can the handbrake be safely released.

7. Once you have found the biting point and your feet are still, release the handbrake. What should happen is nothing. The car should remain still. If the car starts moving forward, push the clutch down a fraction. If it starts rolling back, lift the clutch up a fraction. Aim to keep the car perfectly still. Reapply the handbrake and practise this part over and over until you achieve correct control of the pedals, but only for a few seconds at a time so as not to inflict too much wear on the clutch plates.

8. For the actual manoeuvre, go back to number 6, where you found the biting point. Before you move away perform your safety checks. This comprises your moving off observations. Check your mirror, your blind spot over your right shoulder, your mirror again. Signal if necessary.

9. If clear, but only then, release the handbrake. The car will remain still until you lift the clutch up a little bit. When the car starts moving, hold your feet still, or, even better, just press the accelerator a tiny bit more.

10. As the car slowly moves forward, steer to the right, away from the kerb. How much will depend on how close you are to the parked car. Steer enough to get you out and alongside the car and at least three feet away. Aim to be parallel to the vehicle as you drive past it, if possible.

11. Even though you have checked on vehicles coming up from behind, you can see, in this example, how important it is to check oncoming traffic as well. If you intend, or need, to use the other side of the road, remember oncoming traffic has priority over you.

SUMMARY: *Practise finding the biting point and keeping the car still, using the clutch. Never try to pull away on a hill in anything but first gear. The car will stall, and if you're not quick enough, may roll into someone behind you.*

Reversing

Into a Side Road on the Left

1. Select a safe place to stop. This entails checking that the side road you are reversing into is clear and that the road you are on isn't too busy.

2. Stop, just over a foot from the kerb, but not too far forward of the corner, and note where the edge of the kerb comes up to on the window.

3. Look at the corner. Is it sharp or is it gentle?

4. Check all around and make sure there isn't any other traffic about.

5. Move back SLOWLY in a straight line. Control the speed of the car with the clutch. If you are moving too fast, push the clutch down slightly.

6. As you move backwards, the kerb will appear to move across the window. Judging when to steer (left lock) and how much, is a matter of practice, but you will soon get the idea. As a general guide, on a gentle sweeping corner, wait until the kerb edge is almost in the right hand corner of the back window. On a very sharp corner (90 degrees) wait until you see the edge of the kerb in the right hand side window, directly above the rear wheel.

7. Gentle corners need little steering. Sharp corners need almost full left lock.

8. Just before the front of your car swings out, look over your right shoulder and down the road you are leaving. It isn't necessary to stop unless a car is approaching. This is because most of your observation will be out of the rear window. As you turn, the whole area of road behind you becomes your blind spot.

9. Keep reversing until the kerb edge comes back across the window, almost to the point you first noticed it. Undo

the lock on the steering. The car will need to be moving very slowly to allow time for this.

10. You will need to turn the steering wheel past the point where your wheels are straight again to bring the car parallel with the kerb.

11. Undo this small amount of oversteer and keep reversing slowly, in a straight line, making minor adjustments of the steering where necessary.

12. Observation is vital on this manoeuvre. All other traffic has priority over you. After all, you are moving in the wrong direction, on the wrong side of the road.

13. If anybody comes into the road, stop and give way. If anybody approaches from behind, wishing to turn left or right onto the main road, pull forward and start again when clear.

14. You are allowed to remove your seat belt for reversing, but do this only if you can't manage or see. Remember to put it back on again.

15. The first secret of reversing is to go slowly. This will give you ample time for good observation and reasonable accuracy.

16. PRACTISE, PRACTISE, PRACTISE. For your test and then afterwards for parking and everyday driving.

17. It should be noted here that, on your test, if you go wrong on a reversing manoeuvre, you can do it again. It is more important to put a wrong move right, than to just carry on regardless. If you're going wrong, stop. Do all your observation and pull forward enough to reposition the car correctly. Repeat your observation before moving back again. The examiner wants to see that you think of safety first. Your own safety and that of other drivers, pedestrians and cyclists comes before accuracy of the manoeuvre.

The Turn in the Road

The Three Point Turn

 When turning the car around in the road, what is it important to remember? 1. To complete the turn in three moves. 2. Turn the wheel slowly while the car is moving quickly. 3. Move slowly under control.

A. 3.

NOTE: *If you answered 1, think again. The amount of movements it takes to turn in the road depends on three things: (a) The width of the road. (b) The steering lock available on your vehicle. (c) How well you are able to control the vehicle. The move has become known as the three point turn because the examiner will bring you to a road where he/she knows that you should be able to do the manoeuvre in three. If it takes you more than three turns, it just suggests that you haven't quite mastered the controls of your car. However, in a narrower road it might take five turns.*

1. When instructed, find somewhere convenient to pull up on the left. Make sure you are in a safe position and have good all round visibility.

2. Once again observation is paramount here. Remember, you will be across the road, blocking at least half of it. Everyone else has priority over you, so don't start until the road is clear. No signal is necessary.

3. Move off SLOWLY in first gear and briskly steer right. Aim to have a full right lock by the time your car is a metre from the kerb. Drive across slowly, looking up and down the road again.

4. If someone turns into the road now, keep going or you will block the road completely. Let them pass you once you are on the other side. Check the road and, if safe, indicate that they may pass.

5. One metre from the other side, start to undo some of the lock. Aim to get as much lock off as possible before you stop. Remember that the camber may accelerate your roll into the kerb, so control the car using the footbrake and clutch. As you are now steering left, the front offside wheel will reach the kerb area first. You can then judge how far away you are and stop short.

6. Once stopped, apply the handbrake, so the car doesn't roll forward into the kerb when you release the footbrake.

7. Select reverse gear and bring your clutch pedal up to the 'biting point' (when the engine note drops relative to a specific rev setting).

8. Observation is next. Up and down the road, then over your left shoulder to the far pavement. Release the handbrake.

9. Drive back SLOWLY. Immediately turn the wheel to a full left lock. Look for the kerb over your right shoulder as the rear offside wheel will get there first.

10. One metre from the kerb, start to steer right and take off as much of the left lock as possible. Again, control the car with the brake on the camber. Stop short of the kerb.

11. Apply the handbrake and select first gear. Bring your clutch pedal up to the 'biting point', so that you don't roll back when you release the handbrake.

12. Observation is next. Up and down the road, then over your left shoulder to the pavement. Release the handbrake.

13. Drive across, steering right as much as necessary to get you into your normal driving position on the left. Check your mirror as you move down the road.

14. PRACTISE, before and after your test, in quiet roads.

SUMMARY: *The last metre of road is used to prepare the car for the next movement. Use the whole of the road, stopping short of the kerb (beware of severe camber). Make full observation before each movement. Drive slowly to allow time for your steering and additional observation. Use the handbrake correctly and don't release it until you are sure the car won't roll forwards or backwards.*

1. First movement
2. Second movement
3. Third movement

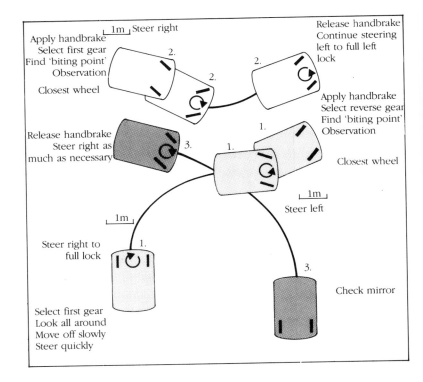

Emergency Stop

If you drive with anticipation and show awareness for the actions of all other road users, you should never have to brake really hard. However, we all make mistakes (some more than others) and so you must be able to stop your car quickly and under full control, should an emergency arise.

It is usually done fairly early on in a driving test because examiners have found that, for some reason, candidates worry about this part of it. However, done properly, an emergency stop is relatively simple.

1. Instruction will be given when you are stationary at the side of the road. The examiner will show you the signal used to indicate that, for example, a young child has run out in front of your car.

2. Move off when instructed (don't forget your observation) and drive normally. Don't drive deliberately slowly.

3. Shortly after checking the road is clear behind, the examiner will give you the signal.

4. Quickly move from the accelerator to the brake. Start to press and gradually press harder and harder. This is called 'progressive braking'. Don't stamp on the brake or you will probably lock all the wheels. Keep on braking until the car stops (unless you skid — see Chapter 46).

5. Just before the car stops, push your clutch pedal down. This keeps the engine running. Leaving de-clutching until the last few feet assists in braking because the engine is also slowing down. Engine braking will last until you separate the clutch plates.

6. All the while you are stopping, keep both hands firmly on the wheel so that you have complete control over the steering.

7. Once stopped, keep your hands and feet in place for a second. Then apply the handbrake and select neutral. Wait for further instructions.

8. The examiner will say something like, 'Thank you, I won't ask you to do another one, please move off when you're ready'.

9. Select first gear. Observation should be: mirror, blind spots over BOTH shoulders (you're not parked neatly on the left, but in the middle of your driving lane) and mirror again. You are looking for cars, cyclists and pedestrians on both sides. Release the handbrake and move off carefully, if safe.

10. Don't make a point of checking your mirror before stopping in an emergency, there isn't time. Instead rely on previous rear observations — hence the importance of regularly checking your mirrors.

11. Q. What would cause you to fail your test?

A. (a) An uncorrected skid. (b) Taking one or both hands off the wheel before stopping. (c) Applying the handbrake on the move. (d) De-clutching, either at the same time, or before braking.

Remember that, doing it wrong in a real life situation would result in somebody lying injured in the road.

12. Therefore, PRACTISE is the only way to avoid catastrophes. Ensure that you can apply the right amount of pressure to the brake for stopping quickly, under full control, and thus avoid skidding. Always be careful to use a quiet empty road when practising.

Parallel Reverse Parking

1. When instructed, select a safe place to stop on the left, before the area into which you are going to park. Of course, when you park normally you won't do this, but, for the purposes of the test your examiner will want to give you instructions first.

2. The object is to park your car at the kerbside by reversing into the space behind another car within a distance of about two car lengths.

3. Follow normal moving off procedure, pull out into your lane and drive up to the parked car. As you approach, check your mirror before slowing and stopping. You will need to stop parallel to and not more than three feet (1m) from the car. The rear of your car should not be much more than about a foot past the rear of the parked car.

4. Select reverse gear. If there is no chance of you rolling away, hold the car on the footbrake for a few seconds. You shouldn't be in this situation for very long.

5. Check you are in the correct position relative to the other car. Look around for traffic up the road and over both shoulders into your blind spot areas. Keep a special eye out for cyclists or pedestrians who may try to use the gap between you and the parked car, or cross the road behind you.

6. Begin to move back slowly and immediately turn the

wheel slightly to the left. Up to one full turn is all that will be required.

7. As you feel the car alter course you need to watch for three things: (a) The corner of the car around which you are reversing. Be ready to undo some of your steering if you get too close. (b) Traffic coming up behind and from in front of you. (c) Be aware of what is happening to your offside front wing as you turn. It will swing quite a way into the road. Because of (c), look over your right shoulder into the lane behind you just before you straighten up the front wheels.

8. Imagine a position on the kerb between one and two car lengths behind the parked car and when the offside of your car is aiming towards it, straighten your front wheels.

9. The kerb will quickly disappear into the blind spot area below the rear and side windows, so be careful now and continue moving slowly. Watch out for the moment when you clear the corner of the parked car.

10. Put on slight right lock. Check you aren't going to get close to the corner of the other car, then continue to put on full right lock. Your car will swing in towards the kerb.

11. Be ready to undo the right lock just as you notice your car is almost in line with the car in front. This will stop the front of your car swinging all the way into the kerb. Straighten your front wheels.

12. Stop as soon as you are happy with your position (i.e. parallel to and not too far away from the kerb, in line with the other car and not more than two car lengths away).

13. Don't continue driving backwards. Remember you're parking, not reversing round a corner. Apply the handbrake, select neutral and rest. Await the examiner's next instruction.

TIP: *Practise until you can park neatly and accurately, not because you may have to do this on your test, but because you will be required to park somewhere every time you leave your car. Often this will be in the areas allocated in car parks or along a busy high street shopping area where time and space is limited.*

It's a good idea to develop this skill now, while everything is still fresh in your mind. How many people do you know who have been driving for years, yet cruise round and round a shopping area waiting to get a space on the end of a row, because they lack the confidence to park in an otherwise suitable slot?

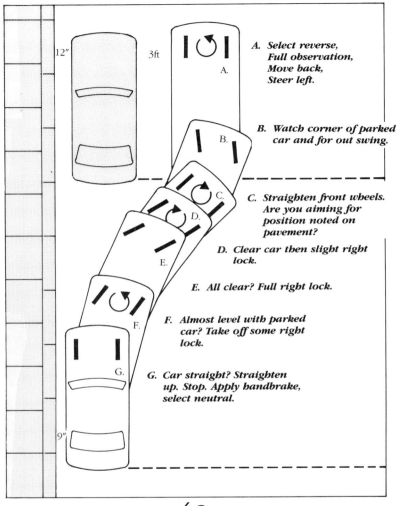

A. Select reverse,
Full observation,
Move back,
Steer left.

B. Watch corner of parked car and for out swing.

C. Straighten front wheels. Are you aiming for position noted on pavement?

D. Clear car then slight right lock.

E. All clear? Full right lock.

F. Almost level with parked car? Take off some right lock.

G. Car straight? Straighten up. Stop. Apply handbrake, select neutral.

49

The Orange Badge Scheme

Disabled persons will be pleased to know that their condition will not normally be a bar to obtaining a driving licence. Some restrictions are placed on invalid carriages, such as driving on motorways, but for the most part, ordinary cars can accept adaptation and be sympathetic to any disability. Adaptation can include automatic transmission, power steering, small selector levers, repositioning of controls and additional mirrors.

Extra time is allowed for you on test, although its content will be the same.

 If you have deteriorating health, what conditions do you need to disclose on your licence application form? 1. Giddiness and fainting. 2. Acne. 3. Blackouts. 4. Diabetes. 5. Epilepsy. 6. A sprained ankle. 7. Strokes. 8. Multiple sclerosis. 9. Parkinson's disease. 10. Any heart disease (angina, coronaries, high blood pressure). 11. Arthritis. 12. Bad eyesight. 13. A missing finger. 14. Mental illness. 15. Alcoholism. 16. Obesity. 17. Cardiac pacemaker fitted. 18. Drug abuse problems. 19. Without hand or foot or use of a limb. 20. A spectacle or contact lens wearer.

A. 1, 3, 4, 5, 7, 8, 9, 10, 11, 12, 14, 15, 17, 18 and 19.

 Disabled drivers enjoy a special parking concession, what is this?

A. First of all, there are often special parking places reserved near to places of importance or interest, so that the driver doesn't have to walk far to enjoy these facilities. Supermarkets, car parks, theatres and hotel areas are just a few. Second, the disabled driver can apply for a parking badge which is orange and easily visible from the roadside. It must be displayed in the windscreen if the driver doesn't want a parking ticket like everybody else. They are usually awarded to drivers who have considerable difficulty walking.   *Rule 141*

 If a disabled driver has difficulty using a seat belt, there is an exemption certificate available. Who awards the certificate? 1. The Department of Transport. 2. A doctor. 3. The police.

A. 2. A disabled driver should apply for the certificate from a doctor.

50

Automatic Cars

Q   What is the main difference between an automatic car and one with manual transmission? 1. There is no clutch pedal. 2. There is no brake pedal. 3. The car drives itself.

A. 1.

Q   What sort of positions does the selector lever cover?

A. N = Neutral. D = Drive. R = Reverse. D1 = Drive 1. D2 = Drive 2. P = Park. L = Lock up.

Q   How many feet do you normally use to drive the car? 1. Both feet. 2. Left foot — brake, right foot — accelerator. 3. One foot.

A. 3. I should use the right foot for accelerator and brake, the same as for a manual gearbox. When manoeuvring at slow speeds (such as parking) it is useful, and safe, to use both feet, one for each pedal.

Q   Explain what P, D1, D2 and L are for?

A. P = Park. This mechanically locks the transmission, and should be used whenever the car is stopped and left.
D1 = Is to select first gear and keep it there. For use in slow moving traffic or down a steep hill.
D2 = Is to select second gear, cutting out first gear. For pulling away smoothly and safely on slippery surfaces, such as snow and ice.
L = Lock up or hold. Enables you to hold the gear already in use, overriding the automatic mechanism, which would otherwise change up to the next gear. Useful for driving down long steep hills or in slow moving traffic. If speed drops, then a lower gear is selected and held.

Q What is meant by 'creep' when applied to automatic transmission? 1. A slick garage salesman. 2. The tendency of the car to move forward. 3. A gear engaging accidentally when in neutral.

A. 2. It is a term which means that the car will move forward just on tick-over, when Drive is selected. It is worse when the choke is used, because tick-over is faster.

Q What does that suggest about your use of the handbrake?

A. It means that I should apply the handbrake whenever I stop, which will counteract the 'creep' tendency.

TIP: *Relying on creep to hold the car in an uphill gradient is bad practice, because if the engine stops, the car will roll back. Use your handbrake.*

Q Passing your driving test in an automatic transmission car means that you can then drive a car with manual transmission. True or false?

A. False. I must take another test for manual transmission.

Q What is meant by 'kick down' when applied to automatic transmission? 1. Selecting the next lowest gear. 2. Checking the tyre pressures with a boot. 3. Movement of the selector lever when it jams.

A. 1.

TIP: *Pressing right down on the accelerator causes a change down to the next lowest gear. This gives you extra power and faster acceleration, very useful when overtaking. This gear will 'hold' until you release the accelerator slightly, when the next highest gear will again come into use, for cruising.*

Q Where should you position the selector lever when towing a car with automatic transmission? 1. Park. 2. Reverse. 3. Drive. 4. Neutral.

A. 4.

51

Car Sympathy

FACT: *You will learn how to drive more quickly if you know a little bit about how your car works, and, knowing how it works, its idiosyncrasies and limitations, will make you a better driver.*

 Which of the following characteristics make a good driver? Concentration, Impetuosity, Experience, Patience, Timidity, Anticipation, Distraction, Responsibility, Doubt, Confidence, Naivety, Generosity.

A. Concentration, Experience, Patience, Anticipation, Responsibility, Confidence.

 A good driver takes only one hand off the wheel to change gear, use necessary controls or give arm signals. True or false?

A. True. The only way to keep control of a moving vehicle is to have at least one hand, and preferably two, on the wheel at all times.

FACT: *As a driver it is important that you recognise the need for regular maintenance and servicing. This will extend the life of your vehicle and save you unexpectedly running up huge garage bills. Neglect of even the simplest checks can result in your vehicle spending much unplanned time off the road.*

Q The servicing frequency for your vehicle is shown in the vehicle handbook. What does it depend on?

A. Mainly on a time or a mileage basis. If I do a lot of miles, then the service may become due before the time duration runs out. If I regularly drive in dusty areas or on motorways then servicing will need to be done more frequently in order to keep the vehicle reliable and safe.

Q There are items on your car that require daily inspection. Which of the following do you think should be checked? 1. Gear box oil. 2. All around the vehicle for obvious faults. 3. Windscreen and windows are clean. 4. Windscreen washer bottle is full. 5. Engine oil. 6. Lights and indicators are working. 7. Brakes are working. 8. Fuel level.

A. 2, 3, 4, 6, 7 and 8.

Q Which of the following should be checked on a weekly basis? 1. Engine oil. 2. Radiator or top up bottle water level. 3. Rear axle oil level. 4. Tyre pressures. 5. Gearbox oil level. 6. Battery electrolyte level. 7. Change contact breaker points. 8. Spark plug gaps. 9. Brake fluid reservoir.

A. 1, 2, 4, 6 and 9.

Q There are warning lights in your car which come on before you start up. If they come on when you are driving along, what do they mean?

A. If the battery warning light comes on, the battery isn't being charged and the most likely cause is a broken fan belt. If the oil pressure warning light comes on, it means that I have lost oil pressure.

Q A rapid rise in engine temperature can be caused by two things. Which? 1. Broken alternator. 2. Broken fan belt. 3. Loss of radiator water.

A. 2 and 3.

TIP: *If either warning light comes on while driving along, pull over as soon as it is possible and safe to do so. There is something seriously wrong and you should not try to drive to a garage or phone. Walk instead.*

Q When do you check the level of engine oil and radiator water? 1. When cold. 2. When hot. 3. After a long drive.

A. 1. Checking either when hot can cause scalding.

FACT: *There are two types of mirrors fitted to most cars, an interior mirror and wing mirrors. However, they don't normally give you the same type of image. Interior mirrors are made of flat glass and this gives you a clear and correct rear view image. Wing mirrors are usually made of curved (convex) glass and this gives you a different view of the area behind your vehicle. Basically, this is to provide a wider field of view, but it also makes it more difficult to accurately judge the position and speed of an approaching vehicle.*

 What does a convex mirror do to the image you are seeing? 1. Makes it seem closer than it really is. 2. Makes it seem further away than it really is. 3. Makes what you see larger than normal.

A. 2. Because of this a car may be closer than I think and it is a good idea to check images in all my mirrors, comparing the different views. Practising will enable me to judge more accurately in future.

TIP: *While learning to drive, take the opportunity to acquire the knowledge necessary to do simple repairs for yourself. Such things as: changing a bulb, changing a wheel, adjusting the fan belt, checking the oil and water, changing wiper blades, dealing with stone chips in the paintwork and cleaning the battery terminals.*

The Parts of Your Car

Accelerator — Controls the speed of the engine. The accelerator pedal is attached to the carburettor.

Air filter — Mounted on the carburettor, it cleans air taken into the engine.

Alternator — Generates electric power for the battery and around the car. Much more efficient than a dynamo at low engine speeds.

Battery — Stores the electric current that will start the vehicle until the generator can take over.

Brake — Uses friction to stop the vehicle. Converts motion of vehicle into heat.

Camshaft — Revolving shaft operating engine valves, giving the power sequence.

Carburettor — Device over the engine which mixes air and petrol in varying amounts.

Choke — Increases fuel in petrol/air mixture. Allows cold starting. Excessive use causes pollution and increased fuel consumption.

Clutch — Mechanical device which separates the engine from the gearbox and hence the road wheels. Allows smooth take up of the drive and gear changing.

Coil — A device for converting the low voltage of the battery to a high voltage (up to 30,000 volts) enough to make a spark jump across the spark plug ends.

Differential — Allows the driven wheels to rotate at different speeds for cornering. Inner wheel travels slower than outer wheel on a corner.

Dipstick — Graduated rod for measuring the quantity of oil in the engine.

Distributor — Device which delivers a high voltage electric current to the spark plugs at the right time.

Fan belt — Belt used to drive fan, water pump and generator. A loose fan belt can cause overheating and a flat battery.

Ignition system — Ultimately produces spark at the plugs. Internal combustion engine — the type of engine fitted to most road vehicles, uses petrol or diesel as a power source. The sequence of events which generates power in your engine is:

Induction — Petrol and air is sucked into a cylinder in the engine.

Compression — This is then compressed into a small space.

Power — The spark plug flashes by arcing an electric charge igniting the mixture.

Exhaust — The burnt gases are then pushed out of the exhaust. There are usually four such cylinders and each one is at a different stage at any given time. This gives you continuous power just when you need it. You can increase the rate (called revolutions or revs) by pressing on the accelerator. Each cylinder houses a piston which moves up and down to draw in, compress or push out the fuel mixture. More accelerator pressure causes the piston to move faster and the sequence to be completed in a shorter time, thus producing more and more power, allowing your vehicle to move faster and faster.

Oil filter — Used to filter out dirt, impurities and metal particles from the lubricating system. A blocked filter has its efficiency reduced and results in increased engine wear.

Overdrive — operates on third and fourth gears on a four speed gearbox. Allows the engine to cruise at higher speeds while doing less work. The car will also lose some acceleration power.

Radiator — A device for dissipating heat generated in the combustion area of the engine. Uses small tubes and fins to create a large surface area through which water is pumped.

Spark plug — A device with two electrodes, one to earth and one carrying a high tension current. A spark ignites the petrol/air mixture in the cylinder.

Thermostat — A device which stops water circulating to the radiator (and thus cooling it down) until the engine warms up.

Brakes

Q There are two types of brakes which may be fitted to your car. What are they? 1. Disc and/or brake pads. 2. Disc and/or drum brakes. 3. Drum and/or brake shoes.

A. 2.

Q Applying pressure on the footbrake slows down which wheels? 1. The front wheels. 2. The rear wheels only. 3. All of the wheels.

A. 3.

Q Where disc brakes and drum brakes are mixed, where would you find the disc brakes? 1. On the front wheels. 2. On the rear wheels. 3. Attached to the handbrake.

A. 1.

Q Disc brakes are more efficient because of which design feature? 1. They get wet in the rain. 2. They cool quicker in the air. 3. They are operated hydraulically.

A. 2.

Q A 'spongy' feel to the brake pedal is usually due to contamination of the brake fluid. What is the likely cause and how can you prevent this happening? 1. Brakes not releasing properly. 2. Air in the system. 3. Hydraulic pressure too high.

A. 2. I should check regularly that there are no leaks in the system and that the fluid reservoir is topped up.

Q When should you apply the handbrake? 1. When stopped. 2. As you stop. 3. Just before you stop.

A. 1. I should hold the car still on the footbrake until I apply the handbrake.

Q How often should you apply the handbrake? 1. Every time you stop. 2. If you are stopped for more than a few seconds. 3. Only when you park or stop at traffic lights.

A. 2. Though I would always apply the handbrake straightaway when stopped on a hill.

TIP: *I usually advise my driving students to count whenever they stop, if they reach three seconds, apply the handbrake until the road is clear enough to move again.*

FACT: *Because the handbrake usually operates only on the two rear wheels, applying it on the move can cause you to skid.*

Q Excessively hard or continuous braking eventually causes a phenomenon called 'brake fade'. What does this mean? 1. The brakes expand and lock the wheels. 2. The brakes 'sweat' and slip. 3. The brakes overheat and are less effective.

A. 3.

NOTE: *This is usually temporary and lasts until the brakes cool again; they do, however, wear away much more quickly when hot.*

Q Some modern cars have dual braking systems. What are they for? 1. One each for hand and footbrake. 2. One for the left wheels and one for the right. 3. Separate systems, one being a backup.

A. 3. If one system leaks there is another system which can deliver hydraulic pressure to the front, rear or both sets of brakes, allowing the vehicle to be stopped safely.

Q If your car pulls to one side when braking, what should you check first? 1. That you don't have a flat tyre. 2. The brake shoes and pads. 3. The steering mechanism.

A. 1.

Tyres

Q How often should you check your tyre pressures? 1. Every other day. 2. Once a week. 3. Whenever you fill up with petrol.

A. 2 should be the maximum duration between checks. It is a good idea to make a point of checking while already in the garage for petrol.

Q If you notice an obvious fault, such as a slow puncture, what should you do about it? 1. Get the tyre repaired or replaced. 2. Pump it up every day. 3. Save it for a spare.

A. 1. It is illegal to drive with tyres which are not properly inflated or have a defect and I should check for obvious faults every day.

Q What instrument do you use to check your tyres? 1. A kick. 2. A thermometer. 3. A pressure gauge. 4. A hydrometer.

A. 3.

Q When checking your tyres, they should be at which temperature level? 1. Cold? 2. Warm? 3. Hot?

A. 1.

TIP: *Always check your owner's manual and keep your tyres at the correct pressures. Over- or under-inflated tyres cause increased running temperatures, uneven and increased wear. This will reduce the road holding capabilities, perhaps with disastrous consequences.*

Q You are driving along a straight road when gradually it becomes increasingly difficult to steer in a straight line. What is probably wrong?

A. The most likely cause is that one of the tyres is going down, perhaps due to a puncture.

FACT: *You should never mix radial and crossply tyres on the same axle.*

Q The minimum tread depth to which you are allowed to run your tyres has been increased to:

0.5mm?   1.2mm?   1.6mm?   2mm?   Circle one.

A. 1.6mm. This means that the central three-quarters of the tread width must have at least 1.6mm of tread depth around the whole circumference.

The Road User & the Law A) 2) Your Vehicle

52
Your Driving Test

Your driving test has three main functions: first, it shows that you can competently control your vehicle under all sorts of different conditions. Second, it allows you to demonstrate that you are a safe and responsible person to hold a driving licence, showing consideration and courtesy to other road users. Third, it shows that you comprehend and can observe the requirements of the Highway Code. In fact, this is all that is required.

Forget all the drivel that you may hear about driving tests. Examiners do not have a weekly or monthly quota of passes and failures. They do not fail everyone on Monday mornings or at any other time. Examiners are very highly trained to carry out their jobs properly and are regularly checked to ensure that you have a fair and unbiased chance of demonstrating your skills as a driver. If you are good enough, you will pass.

I warn all my driving students who are about to take a test that the examiner won't talk very much, except to give directions and to ask them to carry out the set manoeuvres. At the end, there will also be questions on the Highway Code and other motoring matters. Don't be put off by this. Most instructors are talking to you all the time, giving encouragement and traffic information. As your test approaches the 'talk through' should start to become something that you require less and less as your own abilities take over, thus preparing you for your test day. Remember, the aim is for you to eventually drive on your own, without any prompting from anyone. An examiner won't distract you with idle chatter because this increases the chances of your making a mistake. If you subsequently fail, the examiner could be held partly responsible and you would be justified in asking for a free re-test.

Before the Test

Don't apply for the test if your head is spinning with uncertainty. . . ASK! I firmly believe that knowledge equates with confidence and that confidence equates with success.

The test is straightforward enough. Satisfy the examiner that you can drive safely, do the required set manoeuvres, display a thorough knowledge of the Highway Code and you will pass. This book has hopefully gone a very long way to answering many of your questions on all aspects of driving technique, what's expected of you, the law and care of your vehicle. However, some students' questions are of a more personal nature and have to do with general nervous anxieties. Do you have any of these doubts or fears? You may have wondered about some of the following points yourself, but don't be afraid to ask your driving instructor if you have any other worries.

 Will my test be the same as everyone else's?

A. In one respect your test will be unique, just as every lesson you have ever taken was unique — each time, you met different vehicles and traffic conditions and adjusted your driving technique to suit. This won't be a problem for you if you've already successfully dealt with sufficiently diverse road and motoring conditions on your lessons and when practising. But perhaps that's not what you really meant, was it? Please be assured that the content and standard of your test will be the same as the one preceding yours and also the one which follows, the same also as the one in the next town or even the next county. Examiners are fully trained to carry out tests to the same standard and have prepared test routes which are as uniform in content as it is possible to achieve.

Q How do I know for certain that this is true. Don't examiners have bad days?

A. Sure, everybody has bad days, examiners and driving instructors probably more than most. Examiners are closely supervised regularly by a senior examiners' officer. If an officer has been booked to sit in on your test, he (or she) will sit in the back. Don't worry about this or be distracted by it. You are not being examined by two people. Quite the opposite, your examiner is himself (or herself) being examined for professionalism and accuracy, to assure the Department of Transport that the answer to the previous question is indeed true.

Q How do I really know if I'm ready for my test?

A. Have you asked your instructor? Some people could go on having lessons for five years and still feel they need more. The fact is, you never actually stop learning. The point here is: have you learnt enough to pass the test? The question probably has more to do with a state of mind than with ability. Your instructor is the best person to advise you as to whether you have gained sufficient experience, knowledge and skill. He or she can't, however, tell you how to feel about it except to keep encouraging you. Ultimately you have to decide this for yourself.

Do you drive well consistently and with confidence, or do you require regular guidance from your instructor?

Remember, it's a waste of your money and the examiner's time to take your test too early. The money would be better spent on extra driving lessons.

Q How long is the test?

A. In all, about 35 minutes.

Q In what order do I perform the set manoeuvres?

A. There is only one thing that can be guaranteed. That is, the eyesight test comes first. After that the order is up to the examiner and the test route chosen. However, you will normally be asked to do the emergency stop fairly soon after the test begins and you have settled into driving around in typical road and traffic conditions.

Q Should I practise with friends and relatives?

A. If they are over 21 and have held a full UK licence for at least three years, then yes, practise as much as you can. Your driving instructor will advise you when this will be practicable for you and them.

Q Should I practise in the dark?

A. Yes, and on as many different types of road as possible. People who work during the day often have no alternative but to learn in the evening. During the winter this means in the dark.

Q How do I apply for my test?

A. On a driving test appointment application form, number DL26 available from post offices. Fill in the form carefully and post it with your cheque or postal order to the

Clerk of your nearest Traffic Area Office, whose address is on the form. Apply well in advance if you want a specific date. You will be sent a card with the date, time and place of your test. If you can't keep this appointment, you'll need to give at least 10 clear working days notice of cancellation (i.e. 14 days) or you will lose the fee and have to re-apply.

Q What do I need to take with me on my test?

A. Your glasses or contact lenses if you need them. Your provisional driving licence which should be signed in ink. In addition, you will need to make sure that the vehicle you intend to drive is legally and mechanically roadworthy. The required condition of your vehicle is detailed elsewhere in this book. The vehicle must be covered by a current MOT test certificate, if old enough, and you need to be sure that you are fully covered by an insurance policy which allows you to drive this vehicle. A current road fund licence should be displayed in the windscreen and your L plates firmly and correctly positioned to the front and rear of the vehicle.

If you forget any of these points, your test could be cancelled and the fee lost.

The Test Itself

Try to arrive for your test a little early so that you can park somewhere conveniently close. If the test centre has parking spaces set aside for the purpose, use them.

Try to relax for a couple of minutes. Use the opportunity for a final check to make sure that the windows are still spotlessly clean. Walk over to the test centre waiting room. It's helpful to have your instructor or a friend come along for support.

When your time arrives the examiner will call your name. After you have signed the necessary form he will say 'Lead the way to your vehicle, please'. On the way there, you will be asked if you have any disabilities and then the examiner will check that your eyesight is up to the required standard to drive.

This, then, is the first part of the test.

1. *Comply with the requirements of the eyesight test.*

You must be able to read a number plate at 67 or 75ft (20 or 23m) when the letters and numbers are 3⅛ins or 3½ins (8 or 9cms) high. Expect to be shown a vehicle further than this, first. If you can't read it clearly the examiner will let you go nearer, up to the minimum distance. You will not be penalised if you need glasses or contact lenses, so wear them before, during and after your test. An inability to read the number plate indicated will result in automatic failure and loss of the fee. You will have also been committing an offence while driving beforehand. If your prescription is over two years old, it is a good idea to have your eyes checked again, well before your test.

Get into your car and try to get as settled and relaxed as possible. The examiner will join you shortly after checking that the car is in a roadworthy condition and that the L plates are attached properly. Now, first impressions tend to linger and it's a good idea to have the inside of your car clean, especially the seats and seat belts. Seat belts must be in working order, readily adjustable and conform to the law. Remove anything which might fly or roll around in the back and the boot, such as bags, cushions, cases and tools.

Stop lamps and direction indicators must be working properly, as should the other lights, brakes, steering, demisters, windscreen wipers and washers. Tyres should also conform to legal requirements. Prepare yourself for the fact that, if the car breaks down for any reason or the vehicle has been specially adjusted to make manoeuvres easier, your test will be terminated.

The Practical Test

2. *Take proper precautions before starting the engine.*

Before you start the engine make sure you check that the handbrake is on and the gear lever is in neutral. Your examiner doesn't have ESP so don't perform these checks until he gets into the car, when he can see you doing it. If you stall during the test, apply the handbrake, select neutral and start the engine again. Practise this until you can do it relatively quickly, so that you don't hold up traffic at a junction for longer than necessary.

3. *Make proper use of accelerator/clutch/gears/footbrake/handbrake/steering.*

Make proper use of means use the controls smoothly, altering them as and when necessary to suit the road conditions.

Accelerator — Avoid rapid acceleration away from junctions and traffic lights. Use the throttle gently and smoothly, it will respond quickly enough, without racing.

Closely coupled with the accelerator is the *clutch*, and much attention should be paid to co-ordinating their use until you can pull away, change gear and stop smoothly without excessive shudder. Many new students come to me with the idea that the clutch is used simultaneously with the brake. This is a very dangerous practice and a car can soon go out of control when 'coasted'. Coasting is a term which refers to driving with the clutch pedal down or with the gear lever in neutral.

Many people also think that making the car go slowly involves leaving the accelerator alone and just using the clutch. This results in a very juddery crawl which is usually too fast (because the clutch plates grip too much). Instead, set the throttle to a fast tickover and bring the clutch up until the engine note drops (when the clutch plates are just touching). Because the grip between the plates is reduced, control of the car is increased and you can actually go slower than you would if you hadn't set the throttle at all. If the car goes too fast, push the clutch pedal down a tiny bit, if it goes to stop, lift the pedal up a little. Practise in a straight line and then when steering, because this is a very useful form of control to perfect for your manoeuvres.

When you stop anywhere push the clutch pedal down just before the car comes to a halt so that the engine keeps running. If you stop in third or fourth gear push it down slightly earlier than you would in first or second to reduce the chance of judder, but avoid driving for long distances with the clutch down.

Gears — A note about the previous comment — please don't interpret this as meaning you should approach junctions, bends and traffic lights with the clutch down and control the car this way instead of changing down to a lower gear. By all means *stop* in the gear you are in, but on approach to hazards, change down to a gear which matches your speed and the road and traffic conditions, before you get near. This entails looking well ahead and interpreting what you see correctly. Once you have changed gear bring your clutch up so that the car is under control. If you need to change down again, always bring the clutch up whenever you intend to keep moving.

Matching gears to speed is vital if you are to develop an efficient and safe driving system, which demonstrates car sympathy. This means, refrain from changing down too early, so that the engine races when the clutch is brought up and don't leave changing up until the engine rattles.

If you approach a junction slowly in second gear, never 'slip' the clutch to control the car. If your view from the junction is restricted, slow down even more and change into first gear, at something below 10mph. This will give you more time to look before emerging and demonstrates finer control of the car.

When driving uphill, remember your engine is having to work much harder than normal and more throttle will be needed to maintain speed. Change to a lower gear early and delay the upchange slightly to maintain power. When driving down a steep hill, select an appropriate gear at the top to help with braking.

Footbrake — Avoid harsh or sudden braking, which suggests, quite rightly, that you don't look far enough ahead when driving. Smooth, yet progressive braking, spread over a longer distance, produces a more comfortable ride, gives the driver behind a better chance and reduces the chance of you skidding. Never stamp on the brake or the wheels will lock. 'Progressive braking' means gradually pressing harder and harder until you get the effect you want.

Handbrake — Remember to release the handbrake when moving off, and just as importantly, know when to apply it again. Try to use the button and not the ratchet. It's noisy, irritating and will eventually wear away, reducing its 'hold' efficiency.

Apply a handbrake only after the car has stopped (it works only on the two rear wheels) as the wheels could lock and skid. However, you may need to use the handbrake to stop if the footbrake fails for any reason. Apply your handbrake if you are stationary for more than a few seconds and every time you stop on a hill.

Steering — For the most part, keep your hands on the wheel either at 'ten to two' or 'quarter to three'. This gives you full control over your steering, provided you are seated correctly. For turning tight corners at junctions or bends use a push and pull system with big movements of the wheel.

When turning right don't allow your hands, either left or right, to pass 12 or 6 o'clock.

Having gone around, you will now need to straighten up and this is simply a matter of steering left in the same fashion. Don't let the wheel slide back through your hands on its own, feed it back instead.

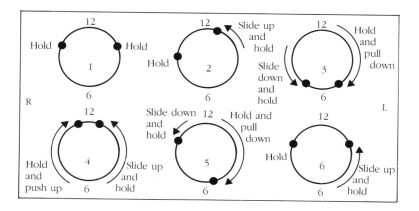

TIP: *Use a washing up bowl or plate to practise turning left and right, but remember that steering a car will require a bit more power.*

Usually, this amount of steering isn't necessary when driving normally. However, on the set manoeuvres and at 90 degree junctions you will need to display your steering skills without crossing your hands. Keeping the car moving slowly is the secret to successful and accurate steering.

Never take both hands off the wheel at the same time. A good driver removes only one hand, and then, just for long enough to operate another control, such as, the gear lever, the rear window demister, lights or to give an arm signal.

Late and early steering will get you into a lot of trouble on sharp corners. When turning right, steering early will cause you to cut the corner and end up on the wrong side of the road. Steering late means you'll probably hit or mount the kerb. Steering early on a left corner could cause your front, but more often your rear, wheel to run over the kerb. Slow down more and steer briskly.

4. *Move away/safely/under control.*

Every time you pull away from the kerb you are responsible for ensuring that you do so safely and without interfering with other road users who are already moving. That means pedestrians, cyclists, motor cyclists and car, bus and lorry drivers.

This will entail you looking ahead and then checking all your mirrors. In addition, the examiner will expect to see you check over your right shoulder, down the side of the car, into your blind spot area. You must signal when necessary to let others know of your intended action. This doesn't mean signal to the row of traffic approaching from behind. You could cause them to brake sharply if they think you're going to pull out suddenly. Instead, wait until the last car has passed, then signal to any other vehicle further back "telling" the driver you intend to move ahead of him. If there is no vehicular traffic around, signal for pedestrians and cyclists, as they need your consideration too.

When moving away keep your speed under control until you are travelling straight again. Don't swing out too far, you will enter the other lane and perhaps cause danger. Demonstrate good co-ordination of your foot controls, handbrake and steering while looking all around.

You will be asked to 'Move off when you are ready' on several occasions during your test. You will be specially asked to perform a 'hill start' and to pull out from behind a parked car, often at the same time, to show that you can control the car in situations of increased difficulty. Remember to check the gradient of the road each time you stop at traffic lights, roundabouts and at junctions, and where necessary, incorporate a 'mini' hillstart into your moving off procedure (See Chapter 48.)

5. Stop the vehicle in an emergency/promptly/under control/ making proper use of front brake.

Soon after the test has started, the examiner will ask you to 'Pull in somewhere convenient on the left'. You will receive an explanation something like this: 'Very shortly, I'm going to ask you to perform an emergency stop. I want you to imagine that a young child has run out in front of you, and stop the car as if there is a real emergency. Do you understand?' Of course, you reply, 'Yes'. Then you will be shown the signal. This could be a tap on the front fascia or window. Take note of it and then 'Move off when you're ready'.

Drive normally and not deliberately slowly. If the examiner feels you are driving slowly because you think you will not stop quickly enough, the signal may be delayed until you reach a reasonable speed. By this time you will probably have forgotten about it and do something wrong in panic. If a car comes up behind you and the stop is cancelled temporarily, the examiner will tell you, so that you don't misunderstand any sudden movements made, like shuffling in his seat or scratching his ear.

TIP: *You should practise the emergency stop at various speeds, in different gears, in dry weather and also in the wet. Your examiner knows that it takes longer to stop at 30mph than it does at 20 or 25mph. So don't think there is a set distance to stop in. You can stop quickly at 70mph, should an emergency arise, it just takes a little longer.*

When you get the signal, stopping *promptly* means: be ready to react quickly and decisively. *Under control* means in a straight line and without locking the wheels. However, if you do skid, you should know how to correct it properly. Keep hold of the wheel. *Making proper use of the front brake* refers to the motorcycle test, but, you could substitute *front* for *foot* because there is a proper way to use your car brakes also. Quickly onto the brake and press harder and harder, progressive braking again. Don't stamp on the brake or press even harder if the wheels lock. Finally, just before the car stops, push the clutch pedal down. Normally the examiner will want to see gentle use of the brake during the test, but for this exercise the car will ultimately rock on its suspension as you stop.

Remember, full observations before you move off again.

6. *Reverse into a limited opening either to the right or left/ under control/with due regard for other road users.*

The examiner will ask you to pull over on the left just before the next side road on the left. Don't stop too close, 15m or more away to stay legal. Then you will receive instruction for the manoeuvre, which will be something like: 'Very shortly, I want you to drive past the junction on the left and pull in on the other side. Reverse back around the corner reasonably accurately and keep on reversing until I ask you to stop. Do you understand?' When you reply, 'Yes', he will say, 'Move off when you're ready'. Proper observation before moving off again is important, even if you are concentrating on the manoeuvre. The examiner may choose a sharp or gentle corner, so practise both.

Under control means drive slowly, using your throttle and clutch to control speed. If you are on an uphill gradient, do a reverse hill start to pull away, so that you don't roll forwards.

Steering also comes under good control. Try to keep reasonably close to the kerb, but not so close that you can't correct marginal errors. If you really make a hash of it, pull forward and do it again (see Chapter 48).

With due regard for other road users means, show consideration and wait if there is traffic, cyclists or pedestrians in the road or stepping off the pavement. Stop if anything approaches. The front of your car will swing out into the road as you turn. An approaching driver has probably seen you and made allowances, but may not allow for your continually altering position if you don't stop.

If you take your test in a van without side windows, you will be asked to reverse around a right hand corner. Your control and use of mirrors is even more important because of reduced visibility. Plenty of practice will help you to do this accurately and carefully.

7. *Reverse parking.*

From 1 April 1991 an additional set manoeuvre was added to the test requirements. The examiner has the option to include this in your driving test if the opportunity presents itself on the test route used. However, you will be asked to do this instead of another manoeuvre, such as reversing around a corner or the turning in the road.

Now, you're not actually going to park between two cars, but reverse park behind one car, and you must do it *under control/with due regard for other road users.*

The examiner, having spotted the car some way off, will ask you to pull in somewhere convenient on the left. To draw your attention to the vehicle, the examiner will say something like: 'Up ahead of you is the parked vehicle I'd like you to reverse behind. Pull up alongside and reverse park into the space, finishing no more than two car lengths behind it. Do you understand?' You reply, 'Yes'. And he will say, 'Move off when you are ready'.

Under control means drive slowly, use the accelerator and clutch to keep your speed down and continually assess your accuracy. Keep a close eye on the corner of the vehicle you are steering around and your positioning in relation to the kerb.

If this exercise worries you at all, practise until you have acquired sufficient skill. You'll be very surprised at a car's manoeuvrability when driven in reverse gear. A little steering has a large effect and this is used to advantage when parking. Give yourself time to see and correct any mistakes. Try not to touch the kerb when you park or worse still, mount the kerb. Scraping your tyre side walls against a kerbstone weakens them and could cause you to have a serious accident if they should later 'blow out' at higher speeds. Practise until you can finish up about two car lengths behind and not too far from the kerb. Straighten your wheels and finish parallel with the kerb, somewhere between 6 and 12ins away.

With due regard for other road users means manoeuvre safely showing consideration for traffic, cyclists and pedestrians. Don't attempt to pull away until the road is clear, because you will need time to complete the manoeuvre. Good observation is vital here. You will have pulled up alongside the car and in a fairly narrow road, there will be no room for anyone to pass you until you've finished.

So, what do you do if another car comes up behind you? Well, there are several options here, some of which may be beyond your control. First of all stop and wait to see the response of the other driver. After all, you are reversing against the flow of traffic. Even if the road is wide, your front offside wing will swing further into the other lane.

(a) In a wide road the other driver may not even give you the chance to respond and just pull out around you, carrying on down the road. This is the reason for stopping yourself. However, you may then carry on, after completing your all round observation checks.

(b) In a relatively narrow road, the examiner may decide for you. The manoeuvre could be cancelled and substituted with one of the others a bit further on. He will tell you of the cancellation and ask you to 'move off when you're ready'. This could happen if a car or cars drive into the parking space you are going to use.

(c) You may have to decide. In fact, the decision ought to be yours. If a car pulls up right behind you, not allowing you room to reverse, then of course you have no choice but to abort the manoeuvre. If the car hangs back and allows you plenty of room, then obviously the driver is willing to wait for you. Perform your manoeuvre as quickly and accurately as you can but without sacrificing safety. If possible, show your appreciation and acknowledge the courtesy of the other driver, maybe with a hand salute.

8. *Turn round by means of forward and reverse gears/ under control/with due regard for other road users.*

The examiner will direct you into a fairly wide and quiet road at some point and ask you to pull over somewhere convenient. You will be expected to show how well you can control the car in a restricted area. The examiner will say something like: 'Very shortly, I'd like you to turn the car about in the road, using your forward and reverse gears, so that we face the other way. Do you understand?' 'Yes.' 'Continue when you're ready.'

Under control means smoothly and slowly with brisk turns of the wheel. Carefully co-ordinate your use of the throttle and clutch to control the speed. When you stop on either side, apply the handbrake so that you don't roll on the road camber and hit the kerb. Practise 'mini' reverse and forward hill starts for this, finding your clutch biting point before releasing the handbrake again. Use the full lock of your steering for the forward and reverse move, remembering to undo some of it just before you reach the kerb. Done properly, you will need very little steering, if any, to go forward again. On the other hand, if the road is narrower than normal, perhaps due to congestion, you may need to go forward and reverse again before driving down the road (a five point turn instead of three).

With due regard for other road users means manoeuvre safely. Look for pedestrians up and down the pavement and coordinate the manoeuvre so you don't meet at the same point. Look up and down the road for other drivers and cyclists and don't start until the road is clear. Stop on either side if a vehicle approaches and let it pass before moving again.

Use the whole of the road for your move but try not to touch the kerb or overhang the pavement.

9. *Make effective use of mirrors well before:*
Take effective rear observations well before:
signalling/changing direction/slowing down or stopping.

I am very often asked: 'Should I have the mirror positioned so I have to move my head when checking?' The answer is 'NO!' Examiners are trained to spot your use of a properly adjusted mirror. Not only because they see your eyes flick, but because your forward movement should be indicative of your rearward observations. In other words, make allowances for the fact that a car is too close or about to overtake you. It's a waste of time just looking. Take notice of what you see and act on it. This is what is meant by *effective use of mirrors*.

Well before means just what it says. Don't leave mirror checks until the last second, look early, and then, if you can, look again just before taking any further action.

Mirrors before signalling. Signalling is a vital part of driving but you must have knowledge of how your signal and subsequent actions are going to affect others. For example, you want to turn right and notice the driver behind is about to overtake you. Refrain; the moment the driver sees your signal he could panic and brake hard or swerve. Let him pass, then signal.

Mirrors before changing direction means when turning left or right at a junction or traffic lights, before moving off from a kerb or traffic lights, overtaking and before pulling in. Changing lanes to the left or right is very dangerous if you don't first check for overtaking vehicles. Mirrors mean more than your interior mirrors. Remember wing mirrors are just as important before changing your course, probably even more so, and don't forget to check again after altering course to ensure you haven't caused a problem for following traffic.

Mirrors before slowing down means check that the car behind isn't too close, in case you need to brake harder than normal. Always check before braking, so that you can spread your slowing down over a longer distance, when necessary. This is important when approaching traffic lights, bends, junctions, pedestrian crossings and other hazards.

Mirrors before stopping. It is easy to forget a mirror check when approaching a crossroads or traffic lights, especially if going straight on, without signalling. The proximity of another vehicle is the reason you should also check before slowing and stopping anywhere.

TIP: *At some point before a test, any student of mine who has a mirror problem (not using enough and when necessary), I ask them to tell me when they use the mirrors by just saying 'Mirror'. This helps tremendously and promotes their proper use in a very short time. Try it if you like, it does make you more aware.*

Take effective rear observations well before refers primarily to motorcycle tests. However, when moving off from the roadside mirrors alone aren't enough and you should also look to the rear. On roundabouts, where you want to turn right and use the inner lane, it is also a good idea to glance over your left shoulder just before you reach your exit and cross the outer lane to leave.

10. *Give signals/where necessary/correctly/in good time.*

What sort of signals can you give? There are three types, indicator signals, arm signals, and often forgotten, brake light signals.

Signals where necessary means give signals when they will help other road users, including pedestrians and cyclists, become aware of your next action. Be warned, making too many signals is confusing and unnecessary. The point of checking your mirrors and looking around is to establish, firstly, whether it is safe for you to do whatever it is you plan to, and secondly, to help you decide if you need a signal to confirm the move.

Arm signals can be used to confirm an indicator signal. For example, if you want to turn right and have just passed a parked vehicle on the left, confirm that the signal wasn't actually for the parked vehicle by giving an arm signal to the following driver.

Give signals correctly means just what it says. An incorrect signal is not only confusing and frustrating, it is downright dangerous. A following driver can react safely only if given a correct signal. Only those shown in the Highway Code should be used. You should refrain from beckoning on pedestrians, either in the street or at crossings, even if you are prepared to stop for them. Another driver may not, and perhaps hasn't read the road as well as you have.

Despite the fact that modern indicators self cancel, slight turns of the wheel may not activate the device and you should always look or listen for the audible warning to make sure any signal has cancelled soon after making any turn. If not, do it manually.

The examiner will be watching to make sure you give correct signals. If you signal right and then turn left, you will fail. However, many learners, probably because they are concentrating or are nervous, take a wrong turn (on lessons as well as on test). This doesn't matter too much, provided you signal the way you turn, but try to concentrate harder and if you didn't quite hear, just say 'Please say that again'.

Give signals in good time means allow enough time for the driver behind to react safely. A late signal is useless and dangerous, and watch out for the driver who doesn't signal at all. If he can't be bothered to flick a switch, he is probably a bad driver in other ways too.

A word about brake lights. They are used to signal that you are slowing down or stopping. Like other signals, brake lights should be activated in good time. This entails your recognising and slowing early on approach to hazards and spreading your braking over a longer distance. This will draw the following driver's attention not just to your presence but also to the hazard ahead.

Arm signals aren't required during the test. However, you can impress by giving the correct signal at zebra crossings during the summer, when windows may be open. If not, then you may be asked about them during 'question time' at the end of your test.

11. *Take prompt and appropriate action on all/traffic signs/road markings/traffic lights/the signals of traffic controllers/other road users.*

Taking *prompt and appropriate action* entails your noticing everything going on in front of you. Look well ahead as well as near, acquire as much information about the road ahead as you can, and give yourself time to take the correct action.

When you come upon *traffic signs* think, what does it mean and what should I do about it? If the sign says 'bend to the right' or 'crossroads ahead' act on it, slow down and keep your eyes open. Don't just go blindly on because you've gone this way several times before without incident. At Stop signs, for example, you must stop and check before pulling away again. If you don't, you will fail. You will also fail if you go into a road which has a No Entry sign or the wrong way up a one way street.

Road markings. Look out for them. Arrows indicate appropriate lanes for turning or going straight on. Choose your lane early and don't change suddenly or unnecessarily. Remember to use the correct lane for turning left or right in a one way street.

Take notice of worded road markings, such as 'Slow' or 'Keep clear' and obey them. The examiner is watching to see how much notice you take of signs and road markings and what do you do about them. Increasingly box junctions are used at crossroads to stop them becoming blocked. Don't get caught out, make sure your exit is clear before crossing. Even though you can stop on one to turn right, make sure the only reason you are waiting there is because of oncoming traffic and not because your exit on the right is blocked.

The ability to act correctly at *traffic lights* is an important part of driving, especially in town. Don't approach lights under acceleration. If they change you will have to brake harder than normal to include the higher revs of the engine, and it will seem like an emergency stop. Ease off the throttle and let the revs drop, then if the lights change you can stop gently (on amber and red). This gives a good impression of anticipation. Check the junction on approach and, if clear, drive through under gentle acceleration. If green and the junction is clear, disregard any change once you are so close that to stop would cause danger. If you have to stop at traffic lights, apply the handbrake and select neutral. Watch the opposite lights. You can often see them more easily. Select first gear ready, as you see them change. Green only means go if clear. If the junction is blocked, or if you will block the junction because your exit isn't clear, wait. If the lights are red on approach and you think they will change before you get there, slow down and change down so that you can carry on as soon as you check the junction and the lights change to green.

Signals by traffic controllers include policemen, traffic wardens and school crossing patrols. You must obey their signals or you will fail.

Other road users means noticing their signals and acting on them. Bear in mind that you must be able to anticipate the fact that these signals may be wrong, and make allowances.

12. *Exercise proper care in the use of speed.*

This doesn't just mean drive within and up to the speed limits, though, it does mean don't drive too fast. Traffic, road and weather conditions should also dictate your speed. Get a move on when the road is clear, slow down and change down when you approach a hazard, such as bends, junctions, traffic lights, crossings, animals and so forth. You will not fail if your speed creeps over the prevailing speed limit, but if you continually speed by a larger margin, you *will* fail. You must always be able to stop within the distance you can see to be clear.

It's easy to speed on more open roads, on the outskirts of towns, especially if you are following another car, so keep checking your speedometer at regular intervals. A car in front may start at 20mph, with you a reasonable distance behind. As the driver speeds up, you may find yourself unconsciously increasing speed to catch up, and before you know it both of you are breaking the law. Beware and don't rely on others to do the right thing.

TIP: *Wherever possible, take your test in the car you have learned in. If you learn in your instructor's car and also practise in your own, decide early which you will use. Learners usually find that they drive better in their instructor's car. Listen and learn how the engine sounds at 30mph in third and fourth gears. Even at 28 or 32 you will notice the change in engine noise, as it will sound 'out of tune'.*

13. *Make progress by/driving at a speed appropriate to the road and traffic conditions/avoiding undue hesitancy.*

This seems to be a direct contradiction to 12, but what it means is, keep up with other traffic and don't dawdle or stop needlessly. However, don't keep up if the traffic in front is speeding. This is particularly difficult in cities and large towns where three or four lanes of traffic are zooming by 15mph or more faster than you are. You can help yourself by accelerating briskly and selecting your lane in good time, not getting caught in the left where you have to negotiate parked vehicles at frequent intervals. Look well ahead and concentrate hard. When you need to change lanes or turn right, check that you don't frustrate anyone in the process of overtaking you. If you drive unnecessarily slowly for the conditions you will fail.

Avoid undue hesitancy wherever possible. Practice will help here. At junctions the road doesn't have to be clear to the horizon before you pull out, but make sure you don't cause others to slow down or swerve, especially if they are speeding. If you think it's safe and you can accelerate up to a reasonable speed in time — go. Keep an eye on your mirror once you've pulled out, though. At junctions and traffic lights, pull away cleanly and smoothly as soon as it's safe and when clear on a green light. As you approach junctions, good observation and driving sufficiently slowly will help you avoid undue hesitancy by providing information that is impossible to gather if you approach too quickly. You can then keep moving, instead of continually stopping at Give Way junctions. On the other hand, if you need to stop, you are going slow enough to stop gently.

14. *Act properly at road junctions.*

This includes T junctions, forks, crossroads, traffic lights and roundabouts.

Of the set manoeuvres, you will be required to perform only one of each, but, it is necessary to drive through many junctions on your test, whether turning right or left. The examiner will be checking each of these and not just one, so it's important that you adopt the correct procedure and are very conversant with the *Mirror – Signal – Manoeuvre – Position – Speed – Look* routine's (Department of Transport Driving manual). Many test candidates fail over their junction procedure, for one or more of the relevant points of speed, observation or position.

Junction procedure is sub-divided into five separate sections, these are:

i. *Regulate speed correctly on approach.* Slow down on approach to a junction and change down to a gear appropriate for your speed. You need to move into the new road safely and without inconveniencing anyone else or causing an accident. You must stop if you cannot emerge safely. Slowing down gives you time to think and look.

If you have to slow right down because you can't see, select first gear just before the end of the road. At the same time look up and down the new road. Stopping will now require gentle braking if necessary. When turning into a side road, approach with caution, slowing on the brake and selecting an appropriate gear before actually turning. Slowing down early enough will help you keep well into the left without swinging into the right-hand lane.

ii. *Make effective observation before emerging* means look properly BEFORE you get to the end of the road. This applies whether you turn left or right, but, turning right is more dangerous because you have to cross the path of oncoming traffic as well as taking into account any traffic in the lane you want to use.

Good control, accurate assessment and the ability to pull away briskly, without interfering with anyone else often means that you can keep moving while others, not so skilled, will always stop regardless. If you stop at every junction, it suggests, quite rightly, that you don't look early enough. Cyclists and motor cyclists need your special consideration because they are only a fraction as wide as a car and are easy to miss.

If you approach a junction which has reduced visibility because of walls, trees or buildings, stop and look before you pull away. Don't sit there and take a chance if you notice the examiner looking fed up. Edge out very gently until you can see. Be very careful if the road disappears around a corner. Open your window and listen if necessary.

iii. *Position the vehicle correctly before turning left.* Provided you adopt the correct lane position when driving normally, you won't need to alter your road position to turn left. Don't swing out to the right before turning if you are driving a car, and slow down enough so that you can straighten up again without hitting the kerb. Never overtake cyclists or motorcyclists just before turning left and make a special point of checking your nearside wing mirror before turning. In a one way street, use the left lane to turn left.

iv. *Position the vehicle correctly before turning right.* On a normal road, meaning not a narrow one, position your vehicle just left of the centre of the road or about one foot from the white centre line. Always signal before making this move and always check your mirrors in case someone is overtaking you.

If the road is narrow, stay over on the left until clear. Positioning yourself on the right is to allow traffic going straight on to pass on the left and keep moving. In a narrow road this is impossible and therefore pointless. Also vehicles coming from the opposite direction may not have enough room to pass and you will end up blocking the road.

In one way streets and on dual carriageways, you should select the right hand lane early when wishing to turn right. If a vehicle is approaching quickly in the right hand lane, let them pass first as they are probably accelerating while you will want to slow down.

v. *Avoid cutting right hand corners* means don't enter side roads or a main road on the wrong side and don't cut right bends in the road. Go forward far enough so that you enter in the left lane and steer a fraction of a second later on bends so that you stay on your own side of the road, you will also be able to see around the corner further. Drivers who cut corners are both lazy and a danger, to themselves and others. All it takes to turn correctly is to slow down a bit more and steer more briskly.

15. *Overtake/meet/cross the path of/other vehicles safely. Overtake other vehicles safely.*

The main requirement here is that you don't endanger yourself or others by overtaking in an uncontrolled manner. Make sure that you don't pull out when another car is approaching, and don't cut back in so that the car in front has to brake or swerve. Never overtake if you cannot allow sufficient side clearance between yourself and the other car. The other driver may try to move over, perhaps to pass an obstruction which you can't see. Always check the road behind first (someone may be overtaking you), signal clearly and move out early. Accelerate past quickly. Dropping down a gear beforehand helps if you're not already going faster than its range.

Give cyclists the same consideration you would a car and don't try to squeeze past just because they're tucked in nicely on the left. Remember, if they hit the kerb or a drain, they may swerve out in front of you. Give them plenty of room and if you are in any doubt about overtaking, don't try it. Never overtake the moving vehicle nearest to a pedestrian crossing or inside the zig-zag area.

Meet other vehicles safely refers to vehicles approaching from the opposite direction. Don't allow yourself to become boxed in or pass so close that wing mirrors or sides clash. Look well ahead for a road narrowing or any obstruction, such as parked vehicles, which amount to the same thing. Slow down on approach and select an appropriate gear for your speed. Thinking ahead and slowing early enough can mean that any approaching vehicle will be clear of the obstruction before you get too near. You can then make use of the gap and accelerate through. Always anticipate trouble and be ready to give way, even if the obstruction is on the other side. If you need to give way, stop well back so you can move out again easily.

Cross the path of other vehicles safely chiefly refers to turning right. You should never hinder or frustrate approaching traffic, causing them to stop, brake or swerve in order for you to cross in front of them. If you can use a gap safely, pulling away cleanly and smoothly, fine — go in, but, if you're in any doubt about it, wait until there is a bigger gap.

If you are positioned correctly for the turn, you are quite safe to wait and won't hold up other traffic unnecessarily. It is often bad positioning which makes learners nervous and take chances. This may not result in an accident, but the examiner may feel the move to be potentially dangerous.

16. *Position the vehicle correctly during normal driving.*

The examiner will expect to see you keep left except for turning right, changing lanes or overtaking stationary or moving vehicles. However, this isn't really enough. *Where* on the left you drive is also important. Don't drive in the gutter, dropping down into every drain and manhole cover you can find. On the other hand, don't drive too near the line along the middle of the road. Two or three feet from the kerb is about right.

Many towns have dual-carriageways in estate areas and residents use the left lane to park. Where there are vehicles parked at frequent intervals, use the outside lane instead of weaving in and out. You can move over to the left again if there is a long clear stretch or if vehicles behind want to overtake you.

17. *Allow adequate clearance to stationary vehicles.*

This is to show that you are aware of the dangers associated with stationary vehicles. Adequate clearance means plenty of room, that is, at least three feet. This allows for a door to open suddenly, a child running out, a pedestrian crossing the road or a car pulling away from the kerb.

Don't forget this also applies to vehicles parked on the right. Where there are cars parked on both sides in a narrow road, drive down the middle and drive slowly. Keep over to the left if there is room in the road for four cars, i.e. two moving and two parked.

Where the road is wide enough, you may pass parked vehicles on your own side of the road, even if another vehicle is coming the other way. Provided there is room, you slow down to a speed which enables you to stop quickly and you keep a sharp look out. Where the road isn't wide enough, it is your responsibility to give way to oncoming traffic. Therefore, stop far enough back so you can pass with a safe margin. If you pass parked vehicles so close or cut in so early that another layer of paint would result in an accident, you will fail.

18. *Take appropriate action at pedestrian crossings.*

Zebra crossings — If there are no pedestrians near the crossing, keep going. Where there are pedestrians waiting at the crossing, slow down or stop as necessary, so they can cross safely. Spread your braking out over a longer distance so you don't frighten anybody on the crossing by braking hard at the last second. Don't sound your horn or wave pedestrians across. Where there are people waiting at the crossing, slow down early and anticipate their stepping out. Pedestrians, particularly the elderly will feel safer if you don't rev your engine or creep forward slowly. If there is traffic behind, you should give a slowing down arm signal so that others know why you are slowing down and don't try to overtake you.

Pelican crossings — Immediately you see the lights look to see if anybody is at the crossing. They have probably pressed the button and soon the lights will change. Slow down on approach and be ready to stop. If you slow down early and the lights change, they may well have changed back again and the pedestrian has got across before you get anywhere near, allowing you to keep moving. Don't move on when the lights are red, even if the crossing is clear, the little green man is telling pedestrians they can cross and someone may step out. If the crossing is clear when the amber light flashes then you can proceed.

19. *Select a safe position for normal stops.*

Wherever you stop on the left, or whenever the examiner asks you to pull in, park parallel to the kerb and conveniently close. Apply the handbrake, select neutral and rest your feet. Cancel any signal. You can leave the engine ticking over while the examiner talks to you, but if you have to get out of the car for any reason, switch off the engine first.

Unless the examiner tells you exactly where to stop you will have to use your common sense and choose a safe place. Don't park where you will inconvenience other road users, for example, within 15 yards of a junction, on yellow lines, outside a public or private entrance, opposite another parked vehicle and several other places (Highway Code rules 137 and 140).

Make sure you stop on or just before Stop lines at junctions and traffic lights, not past them.

20. *Show awareness and anticipate the actions of/pedestrians/cyclists/drivers.*

Showing awareness and anticipation means look well ahead and think well ahead. Make mental notes of the changing situations and conditions which you are encountering now, and those you will encounter in the full range of your vision. Know what you are going to do before you meet hazards.

Anticipation means continually trying to predict the future and never being taken by surprise. Always think what's going to, or could, happen next. What could happen if he does this or she does that and what should I do if something goes wrong with my prediction? Can I incorporate into my driving, firstly, my own mistakes, then the mistakes of others and the things that others do which are correct? This is one of the hardest things to do well and it's easy to get caught out. Indeed, some people never really get it right. Getting it wrong usually means braking hard at the last second and this often has a knock-on effect by producing problems of its own. All too often there is an accident.

TIP: *It helps to stay as far away from other vehicles as convenience allows. Always think of safe gaps when following, passing and leading other vehicles.*

Pedestrians. Look out for them and hope they have seen you. Even so, assume they haven't and drive defensively. Try to anticipate a wrong move all the time. Then you will always be ready if they step out in front of you. Children and the elderly find it very difficult to take account of you and so you must help to keep them safe. When turning into another road, give way to pedestrians already crossing in front of you. Be extra careful when passing buses, ice cream vans and children playing on the pavement.

Cyclists. Why parents allow their children out onto busy roads without proper cycle training I shall never understand. It seems that they think simply buying a bike is enough and negates any responsibility for subsequent safety. One way or another children will soon learn that cars are dangerous, but until then, you need to look out for them. Give them a wide berth in case they swerve or wobble, and be extra careful on hills, on roundabouts and at junctions where they may come up on your inside. Be very careful when turning left and don't forget to check for them when you cross a bus or cycle lane.

Drivers. There are very many really careless drivers on our roads and they can cause you many problems if you don't watch them carefully. They race, jump lanes and lights, pass too close, signal late or not at all, brake hard at the last second, overtake you on a bend or near a junction or even on the left and park dangerously. The best thing you can do is keep well behind and look further ahead, so that when they stop dead, you can brake gently and safely.

You also need to keep an eye open for motor cyclists who can make use of gaps in the traffic which a car can't, especially at traffic lights and other hold-ups.

They will generally be travelling faster than you in many conditions and are much more difficult to see.

During the test you will no doubt notice the examiner making notes on your driving. Don't let this 'throw you' or immediately think to yourself you've failed. This may not be the case at all. Minor faults do not result in failure and this may be what the note is about. On the other hand, your driving may be so good that the examiner is writing out a shopping list. Either way, just ignore it and concentrate on what you are doing, not the examiner.

The final part of your test occurs when you are back at the test centre.

21. *Know the Highway Code.*

During the practical part of your test, you will have been required to observe the requirements of the Highway Code. However, the examiner now wants you to recall parts of your Highway Code in words, by answering questions that will be asked.

It really is a waste of time your driving perfectly and then not being able to answer these questions at the end. It is important that you study all of the Highway Code and get somebody to check you on its various parts. A little at a time is better than trying to cram it into a few days before the test. Granted, the Highway Code isn't a work of literary art, but it is full of commonsense rules that you, as a responsible driver, need to know.

There will be questions on other topics, such as skidding, daily checks of items on your car, the importance of correct tyre pressures and perhaps arm signals. There may also be questions on motorway driving even though you haven't had the opportunity to drive on one yet.

Normally, on test, you will make some mistakes which do not automatically mean failure, because they are not actually or potentially dangerous. The examiner may feel it might be a good idea to see you for a second test. The drive was otherwise good and perhaps you were nervous. A quick response with positive answers to the questions at the end, perhaps even on the odd point the examiner feels you weren't quite so good at will reassure him that you have the correct procedure firmly fixed 'upstairs' and the mistake was, and will be, a rare one.

If You Fail

Please don't be put off from trying again, it doesn't mean you are a bad driver all the time. It is my experience that those who pass on their second, third or fourth attempt make better drivers than those who race through their instruction and pass first time. If your failure was due to normally untypical faults, perhaps because of nerves, you may not feel so disheartened, especially when you are aware of what went wrong and understand the reasons.

Because of the delay between tests (currently a minimum of one calendar month) you will have gained so much more beneficial experience of varying traffic situations and will be better prepared to cope when you eventually pass. It will have also been necessary for you to work on certain points and you are much more likely to deal with problems in a confident manner when you have put extra effort into the solution.

One final point, never throw away your Statement of Failure (form DL 24) in disgust. Show your instructor as soon as possible and reassess the test while it is still easily recalled (if you can remember any of it). He/she will be able to help you concentrate on putting these points right for next time and also improve your overall driving capabilities.

If You Pass

Congratulations! You have shown that you are basically a competent and safe driver and can adapt your driving to suit varying conditions on the road. The effort that you have put into your lessons has proved worthwhile, but it has only brought you to the standard necessary to pass a test. Your task over the next few months and years is to acquire as much experience as possible, so that your driving skills improve with time. A pride in your achievement will help you to maintain a good standard.

Take it easy for a while, short drives around your local area and between towns is better than heading for the nearest city centre. Now is the most dangerous time for you to be on your own. You'll probably feel a little apprehensive and nervous to begin with and you will no doubt soon come across situations that you haven't had to cope with previously. L plates will no longer provide you with a reasonable excuse or cover for your mistakes and this new-found freedom may be very short lived if you forget to drive the way you were taught.

As soon as you feel confident enough, drive on a motorway. I would thoroughly recommend that you initially take someone with you who has 'clocked up' many hours of motorway driving. This could be your driving instructor who will be only too pleased to assist you further. The experience is exhilarating and demanding, so, for the first time, just try a couple of junctions, come off and go back the other way. Morning and evening are the busiest times so choose a time in between.

Never drive at a speed that you feel is unsafe for your own abilities. You can pick up more speed as your experience increases. I tell all of my students that any idiot can drive fast, and most don't drive safely at speed, but the secret of being a good driver is knowing when to *slow down*.

You are allowed to drive on your own as soon as you have your much desired 'pass' certificate. However, you are not allowed to sit in as a qualified driver, with a friend who is learning until you are at least 21 years old and have held your full licence for three years. Remember, your new full licence is at risk if you break these new regulations. Besides, with more experience you will be a far better teacher to your learning friend.

Above all, remember that you are in charge of an expensive and potentially dangerous machine. Please be responsible and drive safely at all times. Good luck!

Index